In Him Is Life

In Him Is Life

How Christ Meets Our Deepest Needs

John B. Rogers, Jr.

Augsburg
MINNEAPOLIS

IN HIM IS LIFE
How Christ Meets Our Deepest Needs

Interior design: Linda Crittenden
Cover design: Patricia Boman
Cover art: Sebastiano, "The Raising of Lazarus." Reproduced by courtesy of the
trustees, National Gallery, London.

Library of Congress Cataloging-in-Publication Data

Rogers, John B., 1941-
   In him is life : how Christ meets our deepest needs / John B.
Rogers, Jr.
     p.   cm.
   Includes bibliographical references.
   ISBN 0-8066-2652-6
   1. Jesus Christ—Biography—Devotional literature.   I. Title.
BT306.5.R64   1993
232.9'5—dc20   93-24245
                                     CIP

The paper used in this publication meets the minimum requirements of American National Standard for Information Sciences—Permanence of Paper for Printed Library Materials, ANSI Z329.48-1984.   ∞™

Manufactured in the U.S.A.   AF 9-2652
98   97   96   95   94   1   2   3   4   5   6   7   8   9   10

To my parents
John B. and Mildred H. Rogers
and
to my parents-in-law
Walter and Clara Ann Brown
with love and gratitude

Contents

Preface

Blessed be the God and Father of our Lord Jesus Christ, who has blessed us in Christ with every spiritual blessing in the heavenly places, even as he chose us in him before the foundation of the world, that we should be holy and blameless before him. He destined us in love to be his [children] through Jesus Christ, according to the purpose of his will, to the praise of his glorious grace which he freely bestowed on us in the Beloved. In him we have redemption through his blood, the forgiveness of our trespasses, according to the riches of his grace which he lavished upon us. For he has made known to us in all wisdom and insight the mystery of his will, according to his purpose which he set forth in Christ as a plan for the fulness of time, to unite all things in him, things in heaven and things on earth. . . .
For this reason I bow my knees before the Father, from whom every family in heaven and on earth is named, that according to the riches of his glory he may grant you to be strengthened with might through his Spirit in the inner [self], and that Christ may dwell in your hearts through faith; that you, being rooted and grounded in love, may have power to comprehend with all the saints what is the breadth and length and height and depth, and to know the love of Christ which surpasses knowledge, that you may be filled with all the fulness of God.   (EPH. 1:3-10; 3:14-19 RSV)

Through A SERIES of dramatic encounters with Jesus, this book takes the reader on a pilgrimage with him to the foot of the cross and the mouth of the empty tomb. The journey is both theological and pastoral. It begins on the Mount of Transfiguration where we are given our theological bearings. From there, this one whom God identifies as "my Son, my Beloved" will lead us through a gauntlet of deepest human need to where a cross is waiting. That cross is both symbol and fact of the "breadth and length and height and depth" (Eph. 3:18) of God's love for the world and those who dwell therein, and of the ends to which God has gone—even unto death— to bring life to those who "walk in darkness" and in "the valley of the shadow of death." The way of the cross—God's way—brings the Christ of God into contact with all sorts and conditions of women and men and forces: evil, personified by the tempter in the wilderness; pride (Nicodemus); shame (the woman of Samaria); guilt (the woman caught in adultery); tragedy (the man born blind); death (Lazarus); doubt (Thomas). In each encounter, the presence and power of God in Jesus Christ meet and overcome the brokenness and hopelessness that, in one form or another, blight the world and human life. Indeed, each of these encounters is, in its own way, a commentary on John's claim in the magnificent prologue to his Gospel that the Word who was in the beginning with God, and who was God, became flesh and dwelt among us; and that *"in him was life"* (John 1:4).

We need to remember that Christian faith and life are not religious accomplishments built up from below, but a response to the weight and presence of a Life beyond our own from whom and through whom and to whom are all things. As we reflect upon our need for God's grace and truth and light for the living of our days, perhaps we shall ourselves be drawn into these encounters, and so be met by the God who will go as far as we have strayed—to hell and back, if need be—in order to find us and give us life.

1
Christ and the Crowded Ways
The Transfiguration

TWO READINGS:
Genesis 22:1-14
Matthew 17:1-21

> Isaac said . . . "[W]here is the lamb for a burnt
> offering?" Abraham said, "God himself will
> provide the lamb . . . , my son."   GEN. 22:7-8

> "On the mount of the LORD it shall be provided."
>   GEN. 22:14

> And from the cloud a voice said, "This is my Son,
> the Beloved . . . ; listen to him!"   MATT. 17:5b

ONE EVENING after supper, Martin Luther read to his family the story of the near sacrifice of Isaac. "Oh Martin," exclaimed his wife, "God would not ask that of anyone!" Replied Luther gently, "But Katherine, God required it of himself." Before we begin our journey along the way of the cross, we pause between stories of Abraham and the father of the epileptic son, their hearts torn apart, the faith of each taken to the limit at the prospect of giving up his son; and we hear from another Father "who did not withhold his own Son, but gave him up for all of us" (ROM. 8:32).

I.

The story of the transfiguration of Jesus functions in the Gospels to let us know who God is and what God is about in the world. In

11

Matthew, Mark, and Luke, the transfiguration stands *at the close* of Jesus' Galilean ministry, which reached its climax in Peter's confession on the road to Caesarea Philippi, "You are the Christ" (MATT. 16:16 RSV). The transfiguration stands *at the beginning* of Jesus' journey to Jerusalem, which would end with his crucifixion and would clarify for Peter and the others the nature of Jesus' messiahship. We will go with Jesus and the three disciples up the Mount of Transfiguration. From that vantage point, we who read the gospel of God and worship the Christ of God are given assurance that God's own way in the world is the way of a cross. "This one," the strange voice from the cloud says in effect, "who today sets his face toward Jerusalem where a cross is waiting, is my Son, my Beloved, listen to him!" (MATT. 17:5b).

The story is shrouded in mystery, yet fairly shimmers with the brightness of revelation. It tells of an event in light of which all other events, prior and subsequent, are given meaning. Do not look for the significance of the transfiguration in some mystical trance or internal vision or subjective psychological experience. Do not seek some logical explanation of how the sun happened to shine just so on Jesus' face at precisely that moment. This is an account of God breaking into time, exposing Jesus as the one after whom neither nature nor history, neither society nor culture, neither politics nor religion can ever again be regarded from a completely mundane point of view, if ever it had been possible to do so.

II.

Look at the transfiguration more closely now, and in sharper detail: "Jesus took with him Peter and James and John . . . , and led them up a high mountain apart" (MATT. 17:1 RSV).

"Up a high mountain apart." There is more to that little word *apart* than meets the eye. In the chronology of the Gospels, the transfiguration is believed to have coincided with the Feast of Tabernacles (booths), which was celebrated annually in Jerusalem. Recalling the wilderness wandering of the people of God between the Exodus and the conquest of Canaan—forty years of dwelling in tents with no place to call their own—this festival became especially popular in Judaism after the Babylonian Exile, and annually drew numerous pilgrims to Jerusalem from beyond Palestine. It was a great homecoming celebration during which nationalistic feelings under-standably ran high. It was a time of Israel's remembering its past homelessness, and recalling God's gift of a home in the promised land. It was a time for recalling the prophets' visions of all nations coming to Jerusalem to acknowledge the God of Abraham, Isaac, and Jacob. It was a time for recalling the glory of God's people Israel.

Picture that, if you will, in an occupied land. No doubt every Roman garrison in Palestine was reduced to a skeleton crew for that week to allow every soldier who could be spared to be on duty in Jerusalem. Better to increase security and hope for the best than to tell the people they could not have their festival. Thus Pilate and the puppet king Herod held their breath and hoped that Caiaphas, Annas, and the Sadducees could keep the lid on. A "messiah" could hardly pick a better time to make his move. One cannot help won-dering if, back there on the road to Caesarea Philippi, Peter might not have added to his confession an unspoken observation: "You are the Christ (and the Feast of Tabernacles is not far off)." When therefore Jesus began to talk of suffering and being rejected and being killed, Peter swore, "God forbid!"; and Jesus shot back, "Get behind me, Satan! You are a hindrance to me; for you have your mind not on the things of God, but on human things" (see MATT. 16:13-23, paraphrase).

It is significant that before he started for Jerusalem, Jesus took Peter and James and John and led them up a high mountain apart (MATT. 17:1). The transfiguration took place away from the hotbed of nationalistic fervor, of violent revolution, of political oppression. There is a crucial difference between the cause and kingdom of the Lord God Almighty and even the most benevolent imperial power or the noblest of liberation movements. There is a world of difference between the *maintenance* of power by violence (Rome's rule of in-timidation) or the *seizure* of power by violence (the Zealots' rule of revolution) and God's rule of grace, which even today calls into question both established and aspirant powers among us. "Jesus took Peter and James and John and led them up a high mountain apart"—apart from the establishment of church and state, apart from the revolutionaries and zealots. Jesus was not going to be a political messiah by either current or subsequent definitions. Jesus was not going to be identified with or claimed by any movement, nor had he any intention of sanctioning the oppressive status quo. Indeed, Jesus proved to be too threatening for the establishment and too patient for the radicals. He was, and still is, too liberated for the doctrinaire who think they know what God's agenda is, and too mindful of God's purpose for the ideologues who have their own agendas in support of which they are only too happy to co-opt the Christ of God. This should not surprise us, really. As the bearer of the divine presence in human history, as the one in whom God comes personally into the world, Jesus would of course call into question all systems and all powers, political or economic, military or ecclesiastical. The occasion may have been the Feast of Tabernacles in seething Jerusalem, but taking his three most intimate disciples, Jesus ascended a high mountain apart.

> Where cross the crowded ways of life,
> Where sound the cries of race and clan,
> Above the noise of selfish strife,
> We hear your voice, O Son of Man.
>
> "Where Cross the Crowded Ways of Life"
> LUTHERAN BOOK OF WORSHIP, #429

III.

> And he was transfigured before them, and his face
> shone like the sun, and his clothes became
> dazzling white. Suddenly there appeared to them
> Moses and Elijah, talking with him.   MATT. 17:2-3

God broke in and gathered up time and eternity, meaning and purpose, identity and destiny into one moment of clarity and insight. Moses and Elijah here represent not just the Law and the Prophets (the historical and theological tradition of Israel), they are also the forerunners of God the Creator, Judge, and Redeemer who will appear in the fulness of time on the day of the Lord (see AMOS 5:18 and MARK 9:11-12). Radiance and light are the traditional symbols for the divine presence, by way of saying that in Jesus Christ we have to do with God himself. "God was in Christ reconciling the world to himself" and, as we shall see presently, "entrusting to us the message of reconciliation" (2 COR. 5:19 RSV).

First, "Peter said to Jesus, 'Lord, it is good for us to be here; if you wish, I will make three dwellings here, one for you, one for Moses, and one for Elijah'" (MATT. 17:4). In their accounts, Mark and Luke add, apologetically, that Peter did not really know what to say or what he was saying, so shaken was he. Already showing promise as a future church executive, Peter was saying in so many words: "Let's institutionalize this! Let's locate headquarters here! The Mount of Transfiguration—that's even better than Rome or Geneva!" He was still running on, still making his case before the assembly, when "suddenly a bright cloud overshadowed them, and from the cloud a voice said, 'This is my Son, [my] Beloved; with him I am well pleased; listen to him!'" (MATT. 17:5).

The brightness told them that God was present, but as they had long known, no one can see God and live. The brightness therefore shone from within a cloud, symbol of mystery and mercy by which God accommodates himself to our capacity. Then, there was a voice, underscoring both the uniqueness of the bond between Jesus and the Father, and the pathos or suffering of God who has given his Beloved—his one and only. As does the story of Abraham and Isaac, the transfiguration exposes the heart of a father, torn by the gift of his only beloved son for the sake of humanity. "This is my Son, [my] Beloved . . . ; *listen to him!*" says the voice. God bids us listen, for God's way will not be known through our programs and proposals, only through our readiness to receive the Word of God from one who bids us follow him to a cross.

The transfiguration is an event of glory and suffering, of power and weakness, of clarity and mystery, of God with us—the Beyond in the midst of life. No wonder that "when the disciples heard this, they fell on their faces, and were filled with awe" (MATT. 17:6 RSV).

IV.

But Jesus came and touched them, saying, "Get up and do not be afraid." And when they looked up, they saw no one except Jesus himself alone.

MATT. 17:7-8

"Jesus himself alone." Moses and Elijah, along with the cloud of glory, had disappeared; the voice was silent. Jesus only was left to their sight and touch and ear. In their temptation to capture the experience, to hold onto it, to batten it down, to prolong it, to possess it, to remain there, they were left with Jesus himself alone. He is our sufficient guide and companion on the way to and through the valley of the shadow that waits below. In that direction lies Jerusalem, and a cross, to which Jesus now turns his face, and their faces, and ours.

"Jesus himself alone." The phrase speaks of our need for a central trust. The psalmist sings: "It is [God] that made us, and we are his" (PS. 100:3). No system, no ideology can ever content us. Our hearts can only rest in one by whom and for whom we are made and who says to us in person, "Do not be afraid." We are made for another, for the faithfulness and love, the joy and excitement, the vulnerability and ultimate security of a personal commitment to one who is with us and among us and beside us, yet above our lies and hankerings, our greed and our grudges, our cruelty and violence— above the noise of our selfish strife. "They saw no one except Jesus himself alone."

The vision of the glory and the hearing of the voice could not be divorced from him who had taken them up the mountain and who was now alone with them. The three witnesses might well have asked as Edwin Muir imagined in his poem "The Transfiguration":

> Was it a vision?
> Or did we see that day the unseeable
> One glory of the everlasting world
> Perpetually at work, though never seen . . . ?

Then the poet hears them wonder:

> Was the change in us alone,
> And the enormous earth still left forlorn,
> An exile or a prisoner?[1]

V.

We can be grateful that the story, indeed that the gospel, does not end on the Mount of Transfiguration. It never was that Jesus turned his back on the pitiable and urgent need of the valley, or the seething and suffering of the city "where cross the crowded ways of life." Not at all! He will walk through the valley—the valley of tears, the valley of the shadow of death—and he will tread the city streets right on into Caiaphas' court and Pilate's palace and right on out to Golgotha. He will do so, however, on God's terms, not on our terms, and not on the world's terms.

The painting of the transfiguration by Raphael[2] is a profound commentary on the relationship between transfiguration and life. The artist paints both the Mount of Transfiguration and the pain-filled valley to which Jesus and the disciples had to return. The canvas proclaims not just the solitude of the mountain but the great crowd down below, not just Elijah and Moses "in glory" but an epileptic boy and his distraught father torn between faith and doubt, between hope and despair—right where so many of *us* live. The painting calls us to hear not just the reassuring voice from heaven, but the complaint about the weakness and failure of Jesus' disciples whom he had appointed and given "authority over unclean spirits, to cast them out, and to cure every disease and every sickness" (MATT. 10:1). With Christ upon the mountain the three disciples had been in the presence of God; now they came face to face with a demon. Raphael helps us see the sharp contrast between the glorious revelation of the mountain and the despair of the valley.

The two scenes in the Gospel and in the painting are intended to stand together that we may understand the nature of God in Christ, and what God is about in the world. The one whom God approved on the mountaintop is the one through whom God now acts in the valley. He whom God has chosen has power over the demons. Jesus' lordship is not a detached glory, but is relevant and personally, effectively present to even the most sordid human situation. Having come down from the mountain, the disciples in Muir's poem recall:

> And when we went into the town, he with us,
> The lurkers under doorways, murderers,
> With rags tied round their feet for silence, came
> Out of themselves to us and were with us,
> And those who hide within the labyrinth

Of their own loneliness and greatness came,
And those tangled in their own devices,
The silent and the garrulous liars, all
Stepped out of their dungeons and were free.
Reality or vision, this we have seen.[3]

The transfiguration gives us a glimpse of God with us and a foretaste of God's intention for us, but it is not an end in itself. It sheds its light on our vocation in the church as the body of Christ. In Henry Wadsworth Longfellow's *Tales of a Wayside Inn*, "The Theologian's Tale" describes a pious monk who was afraid to leave his prayers because he did not want to miss the presence and vision of God he so ardently desired. At the same time, he could not ignore the claims of the poor. The monk left his cell to feed the hungry, and returned to find Christ waiting, and to hear Christ say, "Hadst thou stayed, I must have fled."[4] The reassurance and the challenge of the transfiguration find a theological echo in Paul's encouraging words to the Corinthians:

For it is the God who said, "Let light shine out of darkness," who has shone in our hearts to give the light of the knowledge of the glory of God in the face of Jesus Christ . . . And all of us, with unveiled faces, seeing the glory of the Lord as though reflected in a mirror, are being transformed into the same image from one degree of glory to another.   2 COR. 4:6; 3:18

At the same time, discipleship owes the transfiguration more than an impatient acknowledgement, more than a cursory nod. The way from the confession at Caesarea Philippi leads, of necessity, to the Mount of Transfiguration. Jesus as the Christ of God is not ours to take and use in the attainment of *our* desires for ourselves or even for others. We are called into *his* service as instruments of his peace and compassion in the world God sent him to redeem. Unless our commitment is clarified and renewed, corrected and undergirded from beyond ourselves, our discipleship will lack focus, direction, and power. As Luther put it in his great hymn:

> Did we in our own strength confide
> Our striving would be losing.
>
> "A Mighty Fortress Is Our God"
> SERVICE BOOK AND HYMNAL, #150

Which is worse: faith in Christ that does not issue in deeds of compassion, and thus proves a fraudulent and counterfeit commitment, or compassion unfed by the power and faithfulness of God, thus running out into drudgery, bitterness, and cynicism? Sadly, the world and the church are filled with numerous failures of each kind.

The transfiguration is little more than a strange story if the person and power and love of Christ remain on a high mountain aloof from human need and all the pain of the world. On the other hand, our striving for justice and righteousness, compassion and peace amounts to little except as it is touched and shaped, carried and corrected, judged and redeemed by him who as true God "became flesh and dwelt among us" (JOHN 1:14 RSV).

Raphael's painting, with its scene of both the mountain and the valley, is the portrayal, in its due proportion, of God with us in life and death and destiny "where cross the crowded ways of life." Indeed, the words of Frank Mason North's familiar hymn written against the backdrop of the desperate slums of lower Manhattan steal on our ear as we gaze at the scene:

> In haunts of wretchedness and need,
> On shadowed thresholds dark with fears,
> From paths where hide the lures of greed,
> We catch the vision of your tears.
>
> From tender childhood's helplessness,
> From human grief and burdened toil,
> From famished souls, from sorrow's stress,
> Your heart has never known recoil.
>
> O Master, from the mountainside
> Make haste to heal these hearts of pain;

Among these restless throngs abide;
Oh, tread the city's streets again;

Till all the world shall learn your love,
And follow where your feet have trod.

"Where Cross the Crowded Ways of Life"
LUTHERAN BOOK OF WORSHIP, #429

VI.

Isaac said to his father Abraham, . . . "Behold, the
fire and the wood; but where is the lamb for a
burnt offering?" Abraham said, "God will provide
himself the lamb for a burnt offering, my son."

GEN. 22:7-8 RSV

Here a father's pain-filled words to his son on Mount Moriah
contain a promise that finds fulfillment on the Mount of Transfiguration where another Father speaks "who did not withhold his
own Son, but gave him up for all of us" (ROM. 8:32).

This is my Son, [my] Beloved; with him I am well
pleased; listen to him!   MATT. 17:5b

From there God in Christ moves intentionally, purposefully, re-
demptively, bringing life—his life—into the valley, and into the city,
and into the corridors of power and politics, and into the strongholds
of death and hell.

Notes

1. Edwin Muir, "The Transfiguration" in *The Oxford Book of Scottish Verse*, eds.
John MacQueen and Tom Scott (Oxford: At the Clarendon Press, 1966), 480.
2. Raphael Sanzio, "The Transfiguration" in Cynthia Pearl Maus, *Christ and the
Fine Arts* (New York: Harper and Bros., 1938), 250–53.
3. Muir, "Transfiguration," 481.
4. Henry Wadsworth Longfellow, *Tales of a Wayside Inn*, cited by George A.
Buttrick, *The Interpreter's Bible*, vol. 7, G. A. Buttrick, ed. (Nashville: Abingdon-
Cokesbury Press, 1951), 463.

2
Beginning with God
The Tempter in the Wilderness

READINGS:
Deuteronomy 8:3-6; 6:4-7; 15:7-8, 10-11;
30:15-20a; 31:8; 32:45-47a[1]
Matthew 4:1-11

> For we . . . have a high priest . . . who in every
> respect has been tested as we are, yet without sin.
>
> HEB. 4:15

> Then Jesus was led up by the Spirit into the
> wilderness to be tempted by the devil.   MATT. 4:1

THE WAY of the cross has numerous starting points. In the chronology of the Synoptic Gospels, it begins with Jesus' descent from the Mount of Transfiguration. Theologically, and in the profoundest sense of all, it begins in the eternal heart of God whose intention "from everlasting to everlasting" is to be "God with us," and who "chose us *in Christ* before the foundation of the world" to be his own (see EPH. 1:4). For the purpose of our pilgrimage in these pages, we begin with a dramatic "flashback" to an encounter that followed hard by Jesus' baptism. It is an encounter that throws an ominous

21

shadow over Jesus' ministry from the outset. The shadow is cruciform. The cross, it seems, was there all along; but then we have always suspected that, have we not? Grace, incarnation, redemption—it is a hazardous business God undertakes for us and for our salvation.

Our first encounter along the way of the cross begins on an ominous note.

> Then Jesus was led up by the Spirit into the
> wilderness to be tempted by the devil.   MATT. 4:1

The Russian novelist Dostoyevsky was quite certain there was nothing anywhere in literature that, for sheer insight, could compare with the account of the temptation of Jesus. He heard in it a word out of eternity, beyond the capability of human imagination and expression. Here the epic of human life unfolds: the struggle to overthrow the tyranny of self, only to find that even our noblest desires—"the common good," "the kingdom of God"—become further occasions for self-assertion and the love of power and prestige and possessions. It is the story of the human struggle to decide about God in light of God's decision about us, and always with this voice in our ear, "*If* you belong to God. . . ."

The temptation of Jesus reminds us, as we begin our pilgrimage along the way of the cross, that we travel in the company of "one who in every respect has been tempted [tested] as we are, yet without sinning" (HEB. 4:15 RSV). Our assumption too often is that *we* are tempted as Jesus was, in our physical appetites, in our desire for acclaim and praise, in our lust for power and possessions. The deeper, more disturbing—yet also more redeeming—insight is that Jesus was "tempted as we are, yet without sinning," without giving in or falling victim as we so often do, without letting the tempter persuade him that something or someone other than God is the end, and indeed the beginning, of life. What is *disturbing* is that like Peter on the road to Caesarea Philippi, our voice sounds more like that of the tempter, calling Christ to be the kind of messiah who meets our expectations, conforms to our desires, serves our purposes. What is *redeeming* is that the one who walks with us along the way of the cross will lead us in the way of grace and life. "Because he himself was tested by what he suffered, he is able to help those who are being tested" (HEB. 2:18).

I.

As Matthew and Luke tell it, the same divine announcement attended Jesus' baptism and transfiguration: "This is my Son, my Beloved." In the account of the baptism, the voice had hardly stopped reverberating when Jesus was led out to grapple with another voice, and with a decision about who he was, or rather, about Whose he was. To whom do life, heart, soul, and will belong? Is my life my own to care for as I please, to do with what I please, to commit to whom I please? Do I belong to myself, or do I belong to Another? The echo sounds from Hebrews, "tested in every respect as we are."

The story says that Jesus fasted forty days and forty nights, a time of discipline and reflection in preparation for what was to become the way of the cross. Afterward he was hungry, which gave the tempter an obvious place to start in on him.[2] *Even the Son of God has to eat, does he not? Besides, if you starve to death here in the wilderness, what will become of the grace and truth, the justice and mercy, the faith, hope, and love that are the agenda of this kingdom of God you've been thinking and praying about for the past month, and that you are supposed to announce and demonstrate when you leave here? You have to live if anybody is going to hear about that, don't you? And for you, the Son of God, what I am proposing would be so easy—if, in fact, you really are the Son of God. Oh, I know what the voice said at your baptism. That's something else you've been struggling with out here, and don't tell me you haven't had your doubts about it either. Well, here's a harmless enough way to find out: "If you are the Son of God, command these stones to become loaves of bread."*

What the tempter really wanted Jesus to do was to put self at the center of life. He had worked this temptation before, and with notable success, on that couple in the Garden of Eden: "Did God say . . . ?" (GEN. 3:1), and it was not long before the focus had shifted from obedience to God to discussion about what God had said, speculation as to what God had meant by it, and suspicion as to why God had said it in the first place. Turn a God-centered life into a self-centered life; perhaps it would work as well on God's so-called new Adam as it had on the first one.

The temptation is, even in matters having to do with God, to begin with the self—to fix attention on one's own concerns and questions, one's own sense of identity and calling as a child of God, one's own physical requirements to be and do what God commands. Surely here Jesus was "tempted as we are." When have we seen or known anyone or any generation that began anywhere else than with self? We see it in two-year-olds who are themselves the center of the only interest they have. Later on we call it "individualism" (rugged or otherwise), "free enterprise," "ambition," "initiative," "determination," "drive," "upward mobility." However we choose to describe self-interest, we build vast empires out of it and huge economic and political systems on the basis of it. Finally, it comes to be the core of a national mind-set.

Jesus' answer reminds us that there must be something, Someone, some Word more claimant than "self." There must be a word that keeps sounding after every invitation to indulge the self has grown hoarse and died away into silence. He had heard such a word in his home, in the synagogue, in shop and marketplace. No doubt he prayed it each night and each day—"when you lie down and when you rise" (DEUT. 6:7). Perhaps, like others in his community, he wore it on his forehead and hung it beside his door on a tiny scroll: "Hear, O Israel: The LORD is our God, the LORD alone. You shall love the LORD your God with all your heart, and with all your soul, and with all your might. And these words . . . shall be upon your heart. . . . If there is among you one who is poor, you shall open your hand to him" (see DEUT. 6:4-6; 15:7-8 paraphrase).

It is a word about Whose we are. It is a word about God who made us; who has a prior, present, and perpetual claim upon us in every situation; and upon whom our life is properly centered. It is a word about God whose claim is the one demand that must be satisfied above all others. This word begins in a call to worship, but goes immediately and without hesitation into ethical and moral commandments whereby God's own justice and righteousness take root and bear fruit in the human character and in the social order. In his hour of trial that word sounded in Jesus and through him: " 'One does not live by bread alone [for self alone, to self alone], but by every word that comes from the mouth of God' " (MATT. 4:4; see also DEUT. 8:3). God is the source of life with whom one begins, to whom one belongs, apart from whom one cannot live no matter how much bread (or fruit!) one eats. That much Jesus got cleared up in the mind of his adversary, and in his own mind, at the very beginning.

II.

Then the devil took him to the holy city and
placed him on the pinnacle of the temple.

MATT. 4:5

Right, then, continued the tempter, *forget the business of stones into bread. What about this: You've been out here trying to sort out this vocation you'll be taking up down there among those masses of people. You're supposed to announce that the kingdom of God is drawing near. That is going to be a tough one, given the dearth of evidence to support any such claim. The kingdom of God—the rule of grace in and over all of life. How did old Isaiah picture it: reverence and righteousness, compassion and equity, faithfulness and fairness—the wolf dwelling with the lamb, the leopard with the goat, the lion and the calf, neither hurting nor destroying in all creation, the earth filled with the knowledge of God as the waters cover the sea? Why, I'll bet you could even get approval to make turning stones into bread, this time for everybody, a part of that whole scene. That would be a lot better for them, and for you, than that cross that is waiting for you in Jerusalem; that is, if this kingdom-talk meets with the kind of resistance I expect it will. You're going to need the people solidly behind you to have any chance at all, you know.*

So then, let's talk about how you might pull it off. I think your best bet to win over those poor wretches down there to this vision of the kingdom of God is to show them a sign. They're always hankering after some sort of eye-opener. They want to be overwhelmed. Very well, work a miracle for them—something they cannot possibly deny. Leap off the pinnacle here. That's exactly the kind of thing they will go for. I know it sounds childish to you; but then, they are children! They feel helpless, overwhelmed by life, afraid, unimportant. Why, they will flock after anybody who will offer them simple answers, visible results, instant gratification. That is the kind of religion that sells! If you doubt it (and if you are the Son of God), just look ahead with your omniscient mind's eye to the late twentieth century, and see what this gospel of yours will become in the hands of the "televangelists," so-called, and in those American mega-churches. Man, they will package it in trite little stories and slick formulas, market it like snake oil as a cure for everything from money problems to marital problems, and turn it into big bucks, big business, and maybe even into a political force. Don't you see? Besides, you would not be doing this for yourself; you would be doing it for them. Oh yes, and if you're worried, it is thoroughly biblical: "He will give his angels charge concerning you"— remember?—"lest you dash your foot against a stone"—right out of the Psalms, ninety-one, verses eleven and twelve if I remember my Bible. Don't begin by thinking of yourself; fair enough, and noble—naive, but noble. Begin by doing something that would benefit all of God's children, your sisters and brothers. Bring in the kingdom of God, including bread for everybody "on the house." Do it—for them. "Love your neighbor as yourself"; it has a certain ring to it, don't you agree?

Of course, the "certain ring" is God's own call to justice and righteousness and compassion. It was to have a prominent place in Jesus' teaching as Matthew presents it: "Seek first the kingdom of God and his righteousness" (see MATT. 6:33). In Jesus' gripping description of the judgment of the nations (MATT. 25:31-46), the one criterion the Son of Man looks for is unselfconscious kindness and compassion. The kingdom of God, however, is something very different from some carefully organized, skillfully managed, efficiently run, well-financed program through which we are inclined to use God and gospel to manipulate events and control people, either for personal gain or political ends. The gospel of the kingdom of God is not first of all about what we should do, but about *what God has done,* and what God is doing and will do to accomplish his purpose in and for the world, through us possibly and preferably, but in spite of us if necessary. When the gospel is thought to consist in or depend upon what we do, then it has become an ideology, often thinly overlaid with a few Bible verses and theological catchwords to give it an aura of sanctity. Meanwhile, Christian worship becomes little more than an opportunity for making one's own statement, and the Christian disciple and Christian community get so caught up in trying to identify and respond to the world's agenda that they fail to press God's agenda on the world.

Come on, Jesus, Son of God—if *that is who you are*—*throw yourself down; get them on your side; the sooner you get this kingdom of God launched, the better, for everybody.* With that, this one "who in every respect has been tested as we are" answered: "It is written, 'Do not put the Lord your God to the test'" (MATT. 4:7; see also DEUT. 6:16). No matter how noble our cause or admirable our ends, we do not co-opt God to serve ourselves. We must not presume to bind God to our wishes and our ways.

III.

God at the center of life; God at the controls of the kingdom—*sounds like you're pretty well sold on Deuteronomy's way of looking at things, given how you keep throwing that book up to me. So that is going to be the gist of your message, is it? Maybe you could get it set to music:*

"Joy to the world, the Lord is come!
Let earth receive its King;
Let ev'ry heart prepare him room
And heav'n and nature sing.

"He rules the world with truth and grace
And makes the nations prove
The glories of his righteousness
And wonders of his love."

"Joy to the World"
LUTHERAN BOOK OF WORSHIP, #39

Since that scenario would take, literally, one hell of a lot of truth and grace, righteousness and love, you will forgive me, I hope, if I have my doubts about it. So said the tempter as this time he

took him to a very high mountain and showed
him all the kingdoms of the world and their
splendor.   MATT. 4:8

This was the payoff. According to Matthew, it was the subtlest of all the temptations.[3] *Very well,* said the tempter, *let us take the kingdom of God for our end and the ways of God (which are higher than our ways, according to Isaiah) as our means. Now, I challenge you: Look down over and among and within all the kingdoms of the world—we can see them all from here: past, present, and future—and tell me, honestly, how you think God's rule of grace will fare. There are the East and the West, China and Japan, the seething continent of Africa, and the boiling pots of Latin America, and don't forget the Arab states and Israel there in the so-called Holy Land. You call that God's dominion? No, Jesus, Son of God, that is mine! Admit it. Admit it, and I'll tell you what: you can have it, all of it. You can have it for a simple bowing of the head and bending of the knee.*

The tempter simply meant that faith in God, tacked up against our kind of world, is ridiculous. *Go into that setup with any idea that the grace of God is going to rule in the hearts and lives of people, and in the affairs of nations, and they will crucify you, along with your preposterous suggestion. Even if you are the Son of God, you need to do something more than trust your Father. You need a political base—a world empire with headquarters in a big city. Why, you could give a whole new meaning to the word* superpower—*if you are the Son of God.*

Obviously, we have come to the supreme and final question about the universe itself, about whose it is and to whom it responds. What is the deepest truth about this world, about the human creature, about the human family? What is the creator like who made and owns and rules this world? Who, as a plain matter-of-fact, does have the upper hand?

Then Jesus said, " 'You shall worship the Lord your God and him only shall you serve' " (MATT. 4:10 RSV). Tested in every respect as we are, Jesus keeps insisting that the world is precisely the kind of place where, for all of evil's sleight of hand, where for all the temptation to take matters into our hands and use God to serve our own ends, the scepter has not been mislaid.

> Though the cause of evil prosper,
> Yet 'tis truth alone is strong;

Though her portion be the scaffold
And upon the throne be wrong,
Yet that scaffold sways the future,
And, behind the dim unknown,
Standeth God within the shadow,
Keeping watch above his own.

"Once to Every Man and Nation"
SERVICE BOOK AND HYMNAL, #547

One cannot help wondering if Jesus were not drawing on his experience in the wilderness when, later on, after healing a man who was possessed by a demon, he told about a strong man (the devil) guarding his palace: "When a strong man, fully armed, guards his castle, his property is safe. But when one stronger than he attacks him and overpowers him, he takes away his armor in which he trusted and divides his plunder" (see LUKE 11:14-23). Notice, Jesus did not say "if" or "suppose" or "perhaps" there comes a stronger one. "*When* one stronger than he attacks him . . . !" That was no frail hope, groping about in the dark, sniffing around for some thread of assurance that evil can be overcome. "*When* one stronger than he attacks him . . . !"

In that certainty, Jesus faced the Roman Empire with its legions and its ruthless power; he faced the religious leaders with their hatred and their stones; he faced the crowds with their indifference and the disciples with their ambition and cowardice—arguing over who was greatest and who would sit in places of honor in the kingdom of God, denying, betraying, forsaking him and fleeing at the last. On his cross, Jesus bore the sport of passersby jeering at him to save himself now if he could. He heard one more temptation spat at him through the thief's gritted teeth, "Are you not the Christ? Save yourself and us!" (LUKE 23:39 RSV). He plunged into the depths of despair, into the valley of the shadow of death, into the very bowels of hell: "My God, my God, why hast thou forsaken me?" (MARK 15:34 RSV). When nothing was left at all, God was left: "Father, into thy hands I commit my spirit!" (LUKE 23:46 RSV)—and there the grip of sin and evil and death was broken, and God's grip held fast.

IV.

To begin our journey with Matthew's story of the temptation of Jesus is a way of reminding ourselves that the gospel of Jesus Christ stands squarely in the way of every tendency to have God on our terms, squarely against every drift of thought that would make Christ conform to our ways and means and ends, squarely against every pattern of conduct that would draw life and love and God into the bundle of self. It is a gospel that does not address itself to some fragmentary end, like the preservation of democracy, or the American way of life, or even of civilization. It is a gospel that resists all attempts to marry it to the religious or political spirit of the age, or equate it with some ideological agenda, however noble, or reduce it to a set of ecclesiastical demands and labels and buzzwords such as "evangelical" or "born again" or even "liberation" or "peace-making" or "inclusiveness" or "renewal." Whenever, in the long movement of the Christian church, the gospel has been used to bolster some tottering economic or political system, or to furnish the blueprint of some new order, or to steamroll the latest agenda of the politicos and pressure groups of church or state, there is a religion that is already secondhand and well on its way into decadence and sterility. In God's world we have to begin with God, by whom and for whom we were made and to whom we belong; and we have to travel God's way under God's direction if we hope to come out in God's kingdom where grace rules and "they neither hurt nor destroy" (see ISA. 11:9). Shortcuts run most often somewhere else as we know only too well.

As we begin our pilgrimage along the way of the cross, law and gospel furnish us with food for thought and for life upon our journey:

"One does not live by bread alone, but by every word that comes from the mouth of God."

"Do not put the Lord your God to the test."

"Worship the Lord your God, and serve only him."

MATT. 4:4, 7, 10; see also DEUT. 8:3; 6:16; 6:13; 6:4

As our companion on the way, the Christ of God, "who in every respect has been tested as we are, yet without sinning," is eager to receive and to answer our prayer:

Thou art the life by which alone we live,
And all our substance and our strength receive;
Sustain us by Thy faith and by Thy power,
And give us strength in every trying hour.

"I Greet Thee, Who My Sure Redeemer Art"

THE PRESBYTERIAN HYMNAL, #457

Notes

1. When read together, these verses furnish an overview and summary of Deuteronomy, which is the theological background against which the temptation of Jesus takes place.

2. This chapter uses extensive dialogue between Jesus and the tempter to expound the theological issues at stake in the temptation story. The technique was suggested to me by Paul Scherer's two sermons on this text from Matthew, "What Have You in View?" in *The Place Where Thou Standest* (New York: Harper and Bros., 1942), 115–20; and "Let God Be God" in *The Word God Sent* (New York: Harper and Row, 1965), 143–52.

3. Luke's account (Luke 4:1-13) reverses the order of the second and third temptations, making the "religious" temptation the climax. Matthew seems more intrigued by the temptations of power and politics. It could well be that Luke's order more accurately reflects the temptations of those of us who are church "professionals."

3
The Man Who Knew Too Much
Nicodemus

TWO READINGS:
Genesis 11:30—12:4
John 3:1-17

> Now the Lord said to Abram, ". . . I will make of
> you a great nation, and I will bless you, and make
> your name great, so that you will be a
> blessing . . . ; and in you all the families of the
> earth shall be blessed." GEN. 12:1-3

> For God so loved the world that he gave his only
> Son . . . in order that the world might be saved
> through him. JOHN 3:16-17

As A "ruler of the Jews," Nicodemus was steeped in the Torah and in the theology of the Hebrew scriptures. In his conversation with Jesus about God and God's Spirit and God's life-giving Word, familiar texts very likely filled his mind as he listened and spoke to this "teacher come from God." Perhaps Nicodemus thought about the creation hymn in Genesis 1: "In the beginning God created the heavens and the earth. The earth was without form and void, and darkness was upon the face of the deep; and the Spirit [wind] of God was moving over the face of the waters" (GEN. 1:1-2 RSV). Perhaps he remembered God's call and promise to childless Abram and his barren wife, Sarai: "Now Sarai was barren; she had no child. . . .

33

Now the LORD said to Abram, 'Go from your country and your kindred and your father's house to the land that I will show you. I will make of you a great nation, . . . and in you all the families of the earth shall be blessed' " (GEN. 11:30; 12:1-3).

Already John has announced that this Word of God that brought creation out of the formless void and brought life and blessing out of the formless void of Sarai's barren womb has in Jesus Christ "become flesh and dwelt among us" (see JOHN 1:1-18). And now in the encounter between Jesus and Nicodemus, the weight and significance of this Word made flesh, full of life and light, full of grace and truth, is brought to bear upon human existence—upon your life and my life, upon each life and every life and all life.

From Genesis to John and on beyond, the Bible bears witness to God's gracious initiative with the world and with human beings. Creation begins with God's word of command—"Let there be . . . and it was so." History begins with God's word of promise—"In you all the families of the earth shall be blessed." The gospel itself begins with God's Word become flesh to dwell among us in person. Christian faith and life begin with God who, in Christ, " 'gives life to the dead and calls into existence the things that do not exist' " (ROM. 4:17). So Jesus said to Nicodemus, "No one can see the kingdom of God without being [begotten] from above" (JOHN 3:3). The very foundation of the cosmos, the very heartbeat of human story, the essence of the gospel, the origin and end of faith and life is the mysterious, personal, steadfast, and invincible love of God in Christ Jesus our Lord. In the encounter between Jesus and Nicodemus, each dimension of God's love is present.

I.

The story of Jesus and Nicodemus speaks first of the mystery of God's love.

Albert Einstein is reported to have said that the most beautiful thing a person can experience is the mysterious, and that a person who can no longer stop to wonder, to stand in awe before the mystery of life, is as good as dead. Anyone reading the story of Nicodemus might well wonder if he was not such a person. Nicodemus came to Jesus as an expert in religion. He was a Pharisee, the most devout of Jews. He was a religious ruler, a member of the Sanhedrin. He was a "teacher of Israel" of some renown.[1] He was thoroughly versed in his subject, and his confidence is reflected in his first words to Jesus, "Rabbi, we know. . . ."

Would it be taking too great liberty with the text to see in Nicodemus an attitude that has lost all sense of mystery, and so to regard him as a representative of our own age? As heirs of the Enlightenment, we have lived for a long time with the unbroken confidence that our capacity to understand our world, to apply our knowledge, and to exercise control in virtually every area of life would lead to the mastery of our problems and the claiming of our destiny. Science is our generation's forte, technology our euphoria, and specialization our folly, as we and our so-called experts begin to think that now we "understand all mysteries and all knowledge" (1 COR. 13:2), or will eventually. "Rabbi, we know. . . ."

Mystery and theology have a difficult time when reason and technique, knowledge and know-how are in the saddle. God, providence, judgment, redemption, resurrection, reverence, faith all tend to get shouldered aside as our generation strides along, elbowing its way past those who have paused to worship or taken time out to pray. The poet e. e. cummings warns of the self-destructive attitude of the technician whom he imagined standing before the mystery of creation with no sense of wonder and reverence, and who

> . . . finding only why
> smashed it into because[2]

When the "how-to" mentality so dominates our lives that it becomes more important to describe things and to organize people than to know them, when it becomes more important to manipulate ideas and to manage situations than to understand them, when we are more concerned with what works than with what matters, then we are at the point of destroying ourselves. When every moral and ethical and political and religious "why" is smashed into "because," we lose touch with that dimension of life which points us beyond ourselves and our techniques. We lose touch with what Dietrich Bonhoeffer called "the Beyond in the midst of life"—the one from whom and through whom and to whom are all things (see ROM.

11:36), the one who claims us but whom we never control, the one who pursues us but whom we never possess, the one to whom we belong, but who is always beyond our understanding. In an age with no wonder left in its soul, we identify with the deep longing of Walt Whitman:

> When I heard the learn'd astronomer,
> When the proofs, the figures, were ranged in
>   columns before me,
> When I was shown the charts and diagrams, to
>   add, divide, and measure time,
> When I sitting heard the astronomer where he
>   lectured with much applause in the lecture-
>   room,
> How soon unaccountable I became tired and sick,
> Till rising and gliding out I wander'd off by myself,
> In the mystical moist night-air, and from time to
>   time,
> Look'd up in perfect silence at the stars.[3]

Nicodemus came to Jesus by night and said, "Rabbi, we know that you are a teacher who has come from God." Jesus spoke to Nicodemus of God. He spoke of God, whose Spirit brooded over chaos and whose command brought order out of it. He spoke of God who looked with favor upon Sarai's barren womb, promising birth and blessing to all the families of the earth. He spoke of God, now present to beget us, literally, to new life. Jesus reminded Nicodemus that as one hears the sound and sees the effect of the wind, but cannot tell from where it comes or to where it goes, so it is with God's word of life and light, of grace and truth. It does not return empty, but accomplishes God's purpose—not to condemn the world, but that the world might be saved. One bewildering word followed another until, with gentle irony, Jesus said, "Are you that [well-known] teacher in Israel, and yet you do not understand this?" One likes to think that, from that day on, Nicodemus rested his knowledge in the mystery of divine truth and grace and love, made flesh in this one "from God," and that he wondered as he watched this wondrous love manifest itself in the even greater mystery of a cross and an empty tomb (see JOHN 19:38-42).

II.

Again, the story of Jesus and Nicodemus reminds us that the love of God is personal—that God as Person loves you as the person you are.

Blaise Pascal, the seventeenth-century French mathematician and philosopher, is reported to have said that he never knew a moment's peace until he heard God say, "Relax; your salvation is my affair." Certainly the story of Jesus and Nicodemus reinforces that blessed assurance: not that God is ours, but that we—all of us and each of us—are God's own.

Jesus continually found people who had made a sorry mess of things; and, while he spoke to them forthrightly, without hiding, condoning, or minimizing anything, he did not employ that note of severity that you and I might have used. Almost always Jesus seemed to have felt that what people needed to enable them to pull themselves together and to redeem their aimless, futile, sinful lives was a word of hope and good cheer and encouragement, and this even in cases that to us look callous and hardened and inexcusable. And the amazing results that followed his way with people proved that he was right. The Gospels are crammed with instances, none of them quite the same as any other; for, as someone has said, "The ways of God are as the number of the souls of men and women." God's methods are not stereotyped. Your soul does not belong among anyone else's possessions, nor is your experience to be a mere duplicate of anyone else's experience.

Jesus' use of the birth metaphor with Nicodemus was conscious, calculated, and crucial. Birth is an event of uniqueness and of utter dependence. On the one hand, Jesus' metaphor means that God's relationship to you is as unique and personal as is your physical birth. God says to you, "Fear not; I have redeemed you. I have called you by name; you are mine. You are my beloved child" (ISA. 43:1, paraphrase).

On the other hand, this birth metaphor means that God's relationship to you is as independent of your decision and desire as is your physical birth. This passage in John's Gospel is to your life and my life what the story of the virgin birth is to the life of Christ. It reminds us that we are children of God "not of blood or of the

will of the flesh or of the will of man, but of God" (JOHN 1:13).
Popular usage has turned John 3:3 almost hopelessly into a kind of
command or condition for salvation—"You must be born again," as
if to say, "Now here is what you *have* to do: Go get yourself born
again"—putting the burden of salvation right back on our own
shoulders. Feeling responsibility for his own salvation was Nicodemus' problem to begin with! He fell victim to a theological error
that stands the gospel on its head and misses the point completely.

> For by grace you have been saved through faith,
> and this is not your own doing; it is the gift of
> God—not the result of works, so that no one may
> boast.   EPH. 2:8-9

Jesus, in effect, said to Nicodemus what Pascal later "heard" God
say to him, which word is also God's gracious and personal assurance
to us. "Relax; your salvation is my affair. You are my beloved child.
I love you. I have called you by name. You are mine."

III.

Finally, the story of Jesus and Nicodemus describes the love of
God as steadfast and invincible.

At bottom, Nicodemus' problem was not that he could not find
God or understand God, but that he could not escape God. Indeed,
Nicodemus discovered in this Jesus to whom he was drawn that
night, the God who had come looking for him. Surely it was some
latter-day Nicodemus who, in the nineteenth century, wrote:

> I sought the Lord, and afterward I knew
> He moved my soul to seek him, seeking me;
> It was not I who found, O Savior true;
> No, I was found of thee.
>
> "I Sought the Lord, and Afterward I Knew"
> THE HYMNBOOK, #402

It is small wonder that John's magnificent and moving words
have been called "the gospel in miniature":

> For God so loved the world that he gave his only
> Son, that whoever believes should not perish but

in him have eternal life. For God sent the Son into
the world, not to condemn the world, but that the
world *through him* might be saved.

A free rendering of John 3:16-17,
with prepositional phrases in
italics for emphasis.

In this verse "deep calls to deep" (PS. 42:7); grace is heaped upon
grace (JOHN 1:16). In every phrase are vistas that have no end at all,
but run out beyond the limit of sight, beyond the realm of the mind,
beyond time and space into the mystery of eternity—into the very
heart of God.

John 3:16 discloses the extent of God's love: It reaches to enfold
the world—all *of* it and all *in* it, each and every one; and not only
all people, numerically speaking, but also all sorts and conditions
of men and women. The steadfast and invincible love of God em-
braces the rebels who defy God's commandments, the ingrates who
despise God's goodness, the skeptics and doubters and cynics who
do not even recognize God's existence, the prodigals who turn their
backs on God's steadfast, parental love and make a mess of life. The
prophet Hosea has pictured it as powerfully as possible:

> When Israel was a child, I loved him . . .
> The more I called him, the more he went from
>   me . . .
> Yet it was I who taught him to walk, taking him
>   up in my arms when he fell down . . .
>   bending down to feed and strengthen him . . .
> How can I give you up, O Israel? . . .
> I will not . . . I will not . . . for I am God
>   and not mortal, the Holy One in your midst. . . .

HOSEA 11, paraphrase
of selected verses

Against that image of God, like a father or mother, suffering
the pain of a child's rejection and bearing it in steadfast love, willing
to go to hell and back if necessary rather than give up, the gospel
takes us first to Bethlehem where we walk softly to look into the

strangest cradle we ever saw. Then we go to Calvary where we see the "breadth and length and height and depth" of God's love.

> For God so loved the world that he gave his only
> [beloved] Son. . . .   JOHN 3:16

That verse also discloses the intent of God's love: that his children should not perish, but in Christ have eternal life. "For God sent the Son into the world, not to condemn the world, but that the world might be saved *through him*" (JOHN 3:17 RSV).

Somewhere is the story of an eight-year-old girl consigned to an orphanage as a ward of the state. Painfully shy, unattractive, shunned by other children, regarded as a problem student by her teachers, she had already been transferred from two other "asylums" (as they were called in that day) and now the administration sought some pretext for getting rid of her once again. It was an ironclad rule of the orphanage that any communication from children in the institution to outsiders had to be approved by the director in advance. One afternoon, the little girl was observed stealing down to the main gate and hiding a letter in the branches of an overhanging tree. The director and her assistant hurried down to the gate. Sure enough, the unauthorized note was visible through the branches of the tree. The director pounced on it and tore open the envelope; then, without speaking, passed the contents to her assistant. Scrawled there were these words: "To whoever finds this: I love you."

That story is a tender but faithful pointer to one who was given as God's own Word to the world—who was even hung in full view on a tree outside a city wall for anyone to find. He is God's way of saying to the most casual passerby: to shepherds and kings who crowd around a manger cradle, to soldiers who gamble and criminals who rail and cynics who jeer at the foot of a cross, and even to disciples who, having run away, steal back to watch from afar: "To whoever finds this: I love you!"

Nicodemus knew too much, or at least thought he knew all he needed to know, until Christ found him and took him, like the child of God he was, through long corridors of the Father's house that were new to him, and into great, wide rooms where he had never been. You and I, on our pilgrimage through life, may give him our hand also. For it is for us, too, this mysterious, personal, steadfast, and invincible love of God from which "neither death, nor life, . . . nor things present, nor things to come, . . . nor height, nor depth, nor anything else in all creation, will be able to separate us . . . in Christ Jesus our Lord" (ROM. 8:38-39).

Notes

1. The force of the definite article in the Greek of verse 10 might well allow a translation such as this: "Are you that [well-known] teacher in Israel, and yet you do not understand this?"

2. e. e. cummings, *Poems 1923–1954* (New York: Harcourt, Brace and World, 1923–1959), 404.

3. Walt Whitman, *Leaves of Grass*, Emory Holloway, ed. (New York: The Heritage Press, n.d.), 249.

4
On Belonging to God
The Woman of Samaria

TWO READINGS:
Isaiah 65:1-5,24-25
John 4:5-30,39-42

> I was ready to be sought by those
>   who did not ask for me;
> I was ready to be found by those
>   who did not seek me.
> I said, "Here am I, here am I,"
>   to a nation that did not call on my name.
> I spread out my hands all the day
>   to a rebellious people,
> who walk in a way that is not good,
>   following their own devices; . . .
> who say, "Keep to yourself,
>   do not come near me, for I am set apart from
>   you."
>
> ISA. 65:1-2, 5a RSV

> But the hour is coming, and is now here, when
> the true worshipers will worship the Father in
> spirit and truth, for the Father seeks such as these
> to worship him . . . The woman said to him, "I
> know that Messiah is coming" (who is called
> Christ). "When he comes, he will proclaim all
> things to us." Jesus said to her, "I am he, the one
> who is speaking to you." JOHN 4:23-26

43

IT IS THE SIXTH hour—high noon—the heat of the day. It will not be crowded at the village well at this hour. The women of the village customarily go early to get the day's supply of water. The noonday sun will be uncomfortable, of course, but when you have had five husbands and a lover the knowing, condescending looks, the whispers, the embarrassing silences, the lowered eyes are much more painful. Wait until noon, and you can be alone with your shame, your stained reputation.

Then suddenly there is this stranger. So much for privacy. He is a stranger, though; he will not know you. Besides, he is a Jew; he will not speak, not to a Samaritan, much less to a Samaritan woman. With this stranger, however, there is a word, even for a woman of Samaria.

I.

The stranger's word was, first of all, a puzzling word of grace and life—a word the woman at first could not comprehend. In the repartee at the well, we might characterize the woman, as did one commentator, as "mincing and coy, with a certain light grace."[1] "Will you give me a drink?" asked the stranger. "A Jew asks a drink of a Samaritan woman?" she answered, to which the stranger gave the puzzling reply: "If you knew the gift of God—if you knew who it is that is asking you for a drink—you would have asked, and he would have given you living water" (JOHN 4:10, paraphrase).

If we listen carefully, we can hear over this encounter between Jesus and the woman of Samaria the distant thunder of grace out of eternity:

> And I heard a great voice from the throne saying,
> "Behold, the dwelling of God is with [human
> beings]. He will dwell with them, and they shall be
> his people, and God himself will be with them; he
> will wipe away every tear from their eyes, and
> death shall be no more, neither shall there be
> mourning nor crying nor pain any more. . . . It is
> done! I am the Alpha and the Omega, the
> beginning and the end. To the thirsty I will give

water without price from the fountain of the water
of life."   REV. 21:3-4, 6 RSV

The evangelist suggests that the very Source of life itself—the Word
of God who creates us and claims us as his own possession—has
come in person to say to this woman of Samaria, and to you and
to me, "You are my beloved child." Drink in that fact, Jesus said in
effect, and you can live on it forever.

Like Nicodemus puzzling over how one can enter a second time
into the womb to be born, the uncomprehending Samaritan woman
joked sarcastically with Jesus about how, without a bucket, he is
going to supply this living water. "Sir," she teased, "give me this
water that I may not have to come here—at the sixth hour or any
other time—to draw water." These words from John's prologue fairly
insert themselves at this point in the encounter:

> He was in the world . . . yet the world did not
> know him. He came to his own home, and his
> own people did not accept him. But to all who
> received him [who heard him in faith] . . . he gave
> power to become children of God.
>
> JOHN 1:10-12, paraphrase

The stranger brought to her—indeed, he was for her—God's word
of grace and life. So far, however, she had not heard it.

II.

In this encounter between Jesus and the woman there is, in the
second place, a difficult word of mercy and forgiveness.

Somehow she had been able to relax and banter regarding water
and living water. Was it because she knew that even her well-known
secrets were safe from this stranger? They were safe, by the way,
but not safe *from* him. They were safe *with* him, as she was about
to learn. In the next moment it became clear to her that he knew,
this stranger knew only too well. His tone was abrupt, and hers
became defensive:

> "Go, call your husband, and come here."

"I have no husband."

"Right. Is it because you have just not got around
to it yet?—the ceremony, I mean. Or have you
decided this time—the sixth isn't it?—just not to
bother?"

He knew—five husbands and a lover. But how much did he understand, this stranger? Did he understand the longing, the desperate
need to be loved that had taken her to such lengths—five husbands
and a lover? Did he understand how often she pretended that they
loved her and she loved them? He knew; no secrets from him. This
prophet knew, and was ready to bring the judgment of God upon
her life for what he knew. Prophets are like that. They know so
much and understand so little.

Once again, however, it is the woman who did not understand—
did not understand that her life just as it was, with its longing and
loneliness, was safe with this stranger. He brought her up sharply
and uncomfortably against the facts of her own life. Apparently,
though, he was as willing to drop the subject as she was desperate
to have it dropped. He never said another word about it. She did
not have to be afraid of him. She did not have to steel herself against
the stinging blow of his judgment. He knew her pain. He had come
not to blame her for it, but to bear it for her.

If we listen closely, we can hear again in and over this encounter,
like distant thunder, the longing of God. It echoes from the Old
Testament where, in gripping imagery, the prophet of the restoration
pictures God reaching out to his people:

> I was ready to be sought by those
>   who did not ask for me;
> I was ready to be found by those
>   who did not seek me.
> I said, "Here am I, here am I,"
>   to a nation that did not call on my name.
> I spread out my hands all the day
>   to a rebellious people,
> who walk in a way that is not good,

following their own devices; . . .
who say, "Keep to yourself,
  do not come near me, for I am set apart from
    you."

ISA. 65:1-2, 5a RSV

Apparently, however, the woman was as unwilling to wait for the stranger's word of mercy and forgiveness as she had been unable to hear his word of grace and life. Quickly and skillfully she turned the conversation to religion. How often do we hide from God behind religion? "Our ancestors worshiped on this mountain, but you say that the place where people must worship is in Jerusalem" (JOHN 4:20).

III.

"Very well," said the stranger in effect, "you want to talk about worship. Let's do that. But not at the level of temple cults and rituals, whether on this mountain or on Mount Zion—that is not what worship is finally about; you know that. Worship takes place because God has come to us, claimed us, and called us."

When I come to this part of the story, I am reminded of how my own understanding of worship was, and continues to be, shaped and informed by a clarifying word I encountered early in my ministry. It came in an essay entitled "The Need and Promise of Christian Preaching,"[2] which Karl Barth delivered to a pastors' conference in 1922, some fifty years before I discovered it. It is, in my judgment, a theological exposition of the crucial point Jesus made in his conversation with the woman of Samaria; namely, that worship is called forth from us by God's gracious presence and by God's loving pressure upon our lives.

Barth's suggestion, adapted for effect to the context of our story, is that generation after generation, "on this mountain and in Jerusalem" and all over the world, women and men gather in places of worship to hear proclaimed in one way or another: "God is present!" Here and in Jerusalem and all over, women and men come together and strain to hear, in liturgy and law, in scripture and music, in prayer and proclamation: "God is present!" Here and in Jerusalem and all over, women and men gather and participate in sacrament and ceremony, as if to say: "God is present!" People come and listen and partake; they sing and pray and take part.Why?

Barth suggests the answer is because they have to know: "Is it true?" Is it true, this word about final meaning and eternal purpose in the confusion of our life? Is it true, this news of an ultimate truth amid changing appearances? Is it true, this rumor of a righteousness not off in the far reaches of the cosmos, but present and active within the events that make up our present life? Is it true, this talk of a loving and good God, who is more than a counterfeit deity, fashioned in our image to secure life for us on our own terms, whose rise is so easy to account for, and whose dominion lasts only as long as we can sustain the deception? What the woman at the well and all people want to know and thoroughly understand is: "Is it true?" Is it true that *in* all things, and *with us* in life and death, are grace? forgiveness? God? That is what moves us to worship. We reach out, not knowing what we do, toward the unprecedented possibility of praying, of reading sacred scripture, of speaking, of hearing, of singing about God with and for us.

Seldom is this expressed with such urgency. Of course, people do not go around shouting, "Is it true?"—least of all into the ears of strangers or prophets, ministers or religious folk who always seem to be so sure about everything. But do not be deceived by the silence, your own or someone else's. Among the many and mixed motives that move us to worship—joy and sorrow, hope and fear, gratitude and need—is an intense desire to lay hold of, or to be claimed by, one who overcomes the world because he is its Creator and Redeemer, its Beginning and Ending and Lord. This is what constrains us to worship.

As a minister I do not waste time any longer wondering or worrying about people's motives for coming to church, because I know that down among all the mixed motives and excess baggage that we, all of us, bring to worship is a passionate longing to have the word spoken, and to have the word be true that promises grace in judgment, life in death, the Beyond in the midst of life. A deep hunger for a word from God—that is what really brings us to church, whether we know it or not, whether we admit it or not, or however uncomfortable we would be talking that way about a weekly activity that has become routine and habitual, if not sporadic.

This stranger knew, and so, deep down, do we, that worship is much more than doing the "church" thing or doing your own thing in one or another setting week after week. He knew that worship has to do with the whole of life and thought and action. It has to do with the ultimate source of our existence, the ultimate reason for our living, the ultimate meaning of our dying.

"Perhaps," continued the stranger, "it is because you worship what you do not know that you have to seek solitude here at the well in the noonday sun. Not that being alone gets rid of the longing, the guilt, the confusion, the doubt. If only you knew the gift of God! If only you would hear and understand the word of grace and life, of mercy and forgiveness that claims you as God's own beloved child, you would know that the central fact in worship—the central fact of life and human existence—is not that we are seeking God (either on this mountain or in Jerusalem), but that *God is seeking us*!"

We speak of worship as if it began primarily with us, with our seeking God, with our coming to God. The truth is that in worship we are met by a desire infinitely greater than our own. God desires us. Whatever desire for God we bring to worship from the midst of our living and dying, intense as it may be, pales before that great desire with which God arrives first. So Jesus said to the woman, "But the hour is coming, and is now here, when the true worshipers will worship the Father in spirit and truth, for the Father seeks such as these to worship him" (JOHN 4:23).

The woman was impressed. She looked again at the stranger, and the thought began to gather and form in her mind. This stranger, with clear-sighted eyes that looked so deeply and saw so far, certainly was as she had called him, a prophet. But might he be something more? "I know," she said, surely speaking slowly now, and almost hesitatingly, and all the time watching his face, "that Messiah is coming. . . . When he comes, he will proclaim all things to us" (JOHN 4:25). And Jesus said to her, "I who speak to you am he" (JOHN 4:26 RSV).

Can we stand one more rumble of thunder—God's promise to his exiled children, weeping "by the waters of Babylon"?

> "Therefore my people shall know my name; . . . in
> that day they shall know that it is I who speak;
> here am I."   ISA. 52:6 RSV

As the Gospel of John unfolds, Jesus' revelation to the woman of Samaria is the clearest disclosure of himself he has yet made. Incredibly, he chose this faded failure of a woman. She was, and still is, a rather unlikely person to bring any such good news about a God who knows us, loves us, and who in seeking us will go to any lengths to find us—even so far as to speak to us in person, and to stand with us in every circumstance of life and death. Indeed, in her encounter with the Word made flesh, the grace and life, the mercy and forgiveness of God that at first she resisted now came clear. Running back to the city, she cried out, "Come, see a man who told me all that I ever did! Can this be the Christ?" (JOHN 4:29 RSV). She no longer withdrew instinctively saying, "Keep away from me; leave me alone." Rather, she ran and called others to "come and see. He told me all that I ever did, and still said I was God's beloved child, and that my Father has been looking for me."

"Is there such a one?" asked the Samaritans as they hurried out to the well. Their longing is ours as well, is it not? Is there one who knows us better than we know ourselves? Is there one with whom—not from whom, but with whom—our secrets are safe, our sin noted, judged, forgiven? Is there one who lifts off that guilt that we have been trying so unsuccessfully to throw off? Is there one by whom our deepest needs are held in wisdom and love? Is there one in whom the meaning and purpose of our life are given to us? Is there such a one who seeks people like us who know the experience of guilt and who long to hear the word of grace? Is there one who seeks people like us who know the experience of doubt and who hunger to believe and trust again? Is there one who seeks people like us who know the reality of death and who long to hear the promise of life? Is there one who, in Jesus Christ, seeks us and finds us and completes his own heart's desire by gathering us into the embrace of his steadfast love?

Augustine wrote in his *Confessions*: "O Lord, . . . Thou hast formed us for Thyself; and our hearts are restless until they find rest in Thee."[3] With the woman of Samaria we can confess: "O God, in

Jesus Christ you have made yourself for us; and our restless hearts have been found in you."

"Therefore . . . in that day my people shall know
that it is I who speak to them. I am he."

ISA. 52:6, paraphrase

Notes

1. Cited by Raymond Brown in *The Gospel According to John* (Garden City: Doubleday, 1966). He is quoting from M. J. La grange, *Evangile selon Saint Jean,* 8th ed. (Paris: Gabaldi, 1948), 101.

2. Karl Barth, *The Word of God and the Word of Man* (New York and Evanston: Harper and Row, 1957), 97–135, especially 106–9. This essay provides a background for the discussion of worship on pages 47–49.

3. Philip Schaff, ed. *A Select Library of the Nicene and Post-Nicene Fathers of the Christian Church.* Vol. 1; *The Confessions and Letters of St. Augustine.* Reprint. (Grand Rapids: Eerdmans, 1979), 45.

5
Graven on the Palms of God's Hands

The Woman Caught in Adultery

TWO READINGS:
Isaiah 43:1-5a; 49:14-18
John 8:3-11

Can a woman forget her infant,
  or have no compassion for the child of her
  womb?
Even should she forget,
  yet I will not forget you.
Behold, I have graven you on the palms of my
  hands.

ISA. 49:15-16a, paraphrase RSV

"Teacher, this woman was caught in the very act
of committing adultery. Now in the law Moses
commanded us to stone such women. Now what
do you say?" JOHN 8:4-5

AMONG THE anecdotes concerning the legendary Benjamin Jowett of Baloil College, Oxford, is that once at a faculty reception, an effusive young woman said to him, "Oh doctor, you believe in God; do tell me about it!" The great teacher smiled and replied, "That, my dear lady, is a very unimportant question. What is more significant is that God believes in me." Strange as it may sound to a generation bent on measuring and managing all things on its own terms, the gospel is not fundamentally or finally about our search for God, our thoughts about God, or our belief in God. The gospel is about God's belief in us, God's unending thought of us, God's seeking and finding us.

I.

To say that God believes in us is a down-to-earth way of talking about something the Bible is at great pains to emphasize; namely, God's tireless commitment to his world and to his children. Both Old and New Testaments are rich in metaphors for God, and overwhelmingly these are metaphors that underscore God's relationship to us. Over and again the Bible reminds us that as Creator, Provider, Keeper, Judge, Ruler, Preserver, Redeemer, as one whom we may address in tenderest intimacy as "Abba! Father!" God promises himself to us, gives himself to us, and remains committed to us. However we may perceive God at one time or another in our lives, or even if we do not perceive God at all, God's commitment to us is unshakable.

In the sixth century B.C., to his captive people in Babylon, the prophet, Isaiah of the Exile, offers the ringing reassurance of God's own words:

> Thus says the LORD, he who created you, O Jacob,
>   he who formed you, O Israel:
> "Fear not, for I have redeemed you;
>   I have called you by name, you are mine. . . .
> Because you are precious in my eyes,
>   and honored, and I love you, . . .
> Fear not, for I am with you."
>
> ISA. 43:1, 4a, 5a RSV

That is a word for all seasons, all ages, all people. The Creator of heaven and earth simply wants to remind us that he has made us and that we can count on him not to forget it. God is not going to create human beings and then abandon them to go through life alone and uncared for. It is an especially appropriate word also in which to frame the liturgy for the Sacrament of Holy Baptism, in particular the baptism of an infant. At the moment of baptism the child's name is called, implying that God gives him or her that name and says, in effect, "You are my child, and that is not your doing; it is my choice and my doing!" God believes in us, and until we hear God say to us, "I have called you by name; you are mine," we have not heard the gospel in its fulness.

II.

God believes in us. God made that choice "in the beginning," as Genesis tells it, creating human beings, male and female, "in the image of God" to exercise dominion in the earth on his behalf. That is where God first got involved, and even when to stay involved was painful, God never flinched from this commitment or tried to get out of it. Even when the whole thing seemed to have fallen apart, with humanity scattered in confusion over the face of the earth, God still patiently and persistently set heart, mind, and hand upon a plan to bless—to redeem—"all the families of the earth" (see GEN. 12:1-3).

As that plan unfolded, there was every justification for God's just dropping the whole thing. Abraham, first recipient of the promise of redemption, archetypical believer, role model of faithfulness and trust for future generations, was not only a notorious liar, but also hedged his bets against God's explicit promise—"I will make of you a great nation. Your descendants shall be as the stars of heaven" (see GEN. 12:2; 15:5). In view of Sarah's barrenness, Abraham arranged to have a son by her Egyptian slave, Hagar, just in case God did not, or could not, deliver on so grand a promise. "Abraham believed God," we are told, but to think that Sarah, age ninety, would ever have a child was, well, laughable. Jacob, the promise-bearer, was a deceiver, a cheat, a thief, with his mother Rebekah as an accomplice in a family scam against his older twin Esau and their blind father Isaac. Moses, hero of the Exodus, was a murderer. David, king of Israel par excellence, was an adulterer. Through it all God's commitment persisted in spite of what he had to work with.

The people of God were often no better than their leaders, ready at an instant to embrace a golden calf or a Canaanite fertility god—a predictable, manageable deity—rather than to trust and to wait for and to worship one whose only name was a promise to be there for them, and whose presence was ever-shrouded in mystery. Over and over again, the people turned away "like an adulterous wife," as Jeremiah and Hosea described them, or "like an ungrateful and rebellious child," running roughshod over the tenderest and most sacred of relationships. Oh, it was painful, this recurring rejection, this proud, conscious, willful renunciation of God's love; and given God's sense of justice, the divine anger was surely kindled, the divine patience taken near to exhaustion, God's heart torn apart with grief. All of the emotions are there in the prophetic oracles and in the biblical history—anger, exasperation, disappointment, grief; but none more powerful than the parental compassion that will do anything—plead, scold, brood, withdraw, deprive, strike out—anything but give up. Through now one prophet, now another, God laid bare his heart to reveal the love that would not let them go:

> How can I give you up,
>   Ephraim?
> How can I hand you over,
>   O Israel?   HOS. 11:8

> Is Ephraim my dear son?
>   Is he my darling child?
> For as often as I speak against him,
>   I do remember him still.
> Therefore my heart yearns for him;
>   I will surely have mercy on him,
>   says the LORD.   JER. 31:20 RSV

> Can a woman forget her infant,
>   or have no compassion for the child of her
>   womb?
> Even should she forget,
>   yet I will not forget you.
> Behold, I have graven you on the palms of my
>   hands.   ISA. 49:15-16a, paraphrase

Pick the strongest commitment you can imagine, say these texts— the commitment of a mother to her nursing infant—and God's commitment goes even beyond that, and with the scars to show for it. "Behold, I have graven you on the palms of my hands!"

III.

As helpful as it is to use human commitments as analogies to express God's commitment to us, in deepest truth, and the Bible knows this full well, God loves like God, and not like anyone else. God's love for us, God's commitment to us, finally is unlike anything we can identify in our own experience. The love of a parent may point to or hint at the love of God, but we have only to read the newspaper to be reminded almost daily that some parents abuse children, and torture them, and even kill them. Only God can reveal the love of God, only God can demonstrate the breadth and length and height and depth of the divine commitment to us. That demonstration awaits us on a hill outside the city of Jerusalem where a cross stands out against the evening sky.

That cross waits for one who, along the way that led him there, encountered, reached out, and drew to himself all sorts and conditions of women and men. He welcomed them, talked with them, ate with them, spent time with them as if they were special and precious to him. He told them parables about God's love for them, God's commitment to them, God's belief in them, *and in us.* "Listen," he said, "which one of you, having a hundred sheep and losing one of them, does not leave the ninety-nine in the wilderness and go after the one that is lost until he finds it?" (LUKE 15:3-4). Think about that: No shepherd worth his salt would leave a whole flock untended, untethered in the wilderness to go and look for one missing sheep. He would have no flock at all when he got back. The Good Shepherd, however, sets his love upon each as if there were but one to love. And if, while he looks for the lost one, the ninety-nine others stray, he will go after each one tirelessly *until* he finds them.

"Or what woman," he said, "having ten silver coins, if she loses one of them, does not search for it high and low, and when she finds it has a party to celebrate?" (LUKE 15:8-10, paraphrase). Most of us would not spend lavishly to celebrate the recovery of a small amount of money. God, however, pulls out all the stops—throws everything he has into celebrating the recovery of one who is precious to him.

"A certain man had two sons," he said. Thus did Jesus unfold that best known of all parables about the prodigal who demanded his inheritance, forsook his father, and squandered the money frivolously and foolishly. He had no thought of home until he woke one day, miserably hungry, and hatched up a scheme to go back home where he could get some food in his stomach and clothes on his back. Lo and behold, it worked, and beyond his wildest expectations! His father ran to meet him and flung his arms around him. Before the son could even recite his carefully rehearsed speech about having "sinned against heaven and before you, my father," and about "not being worthy to be called son," he was given new clothes and shoes, and was presented the ring of filial authority that restored him to full status in the family, as if he had never been given his inheritance, much less lost it. His father even threw a banquet to celebrate the return of "my son who was dead, and is alive again; he was lost and is found." (See LUKE 15:11-32.)

To hear afresh the profound word of grace in this too-familiar story, we might imagine that the next morning, still feeling the effects of the late-night party and too much wine, but also too excited over the homecoming to sleep, the father tiptoes to the son's room—they had kept it for him, just as he left it, in case he ever did come home. The father just wants to look in on his sleeping boy. He opens the door ever so carefully and quietly so as not to awaken him. Then he staggers under the blow of his disappointment as he looks upon an empty bed and realizes that the boy is gone again, along with the fine clothes and the new shoes and the expensive ring. From the shadows at the end of the hall the voice of the older brother says, "Well, he's gone again; that's twice now. How many times are you going to let him do this to you; three, five, seven? How many times will you take him back?" And the father, choking on his tears, answers softly, "Seventy times seven."[1] Why? Because "love bears all things, believes all things, hopes all things, endures all things. Love never ends" (1 COR. 13:7-8a). God loves like that, says he who told this parable. God loves like God.

IV.

In the eighth chapter of John, we find Jesus teaching in the temple—perhaps it would not be too much to imagine that he was using these very parables about the lost sheep and the lost coin and the lost son—when the scribes and Pharisees brought to him a woman caught in adultery. Although the story has all the earmarks of an authentic incident from the life of Jesus, it is not in the earliest manuscripts of the Fourth Gospel. It shows up in later editions of both John and Luke, evidence that while none of the evangelists chose originally to include it in their Gospels, it was a story the church simply could not give up. The story is a dramatic illustration of Paul's theme in the magnificent eighth chapter of Romans: "There is therefore now no condemnation for those who are in Christ Jesus. . . . If God is for us, who is against us? . . . [for nothing] in all creation, will be able to separate us from the love of God in Christ Jesus our Lord" (ROM. 8:1,31,39).

There was no condemnation for the scribes and Pharisees. Jesus did not arraign them saying, "There is not a virtuous man among you!" He made each man his own judge. We have all seen people who gnash their teeth with diabolic savageness over the weakness of some poor offender—people whose religion seems to be little more than a license to hate with God on their side. Eagerness to hurry people off to hell is a perversion of the gospel of God worse than any sin of the flesh. Such people may turn red eyes to heaven as if in prayer, but they do not have the spirit of Jesus Christ. Unknown to them are the grace and love and compassion at the heart of God who has graven us—each of us and all of us—on the palms of his hands.

The Koran says that on the day of resurrection the record each of us has compiled will be open before us—our life as an open book. Something like that apparently flashed before the eyes of these men when Jesus invited them to throw the first stone. Conscience, commissioned by divine authority, showed them that the only difference between themselves and the woman was that her sin was found out, and theirs was not—yet. They realized that what they saw as they looked so self-righteously upon this guilty woman was what God sees when he looks upon them—"They went away, one by one, beginning with the eldest" (JOHN 8:9 RSV). Why the eldest first? Do age and experience perhaps temper self-righteousness, broaden understanding, open hearts, and quicken sympathies? "One need only grow old," said Goethe, "to become gentler in one's judgments. I see no fault committed which I could not have committed myself."[2] The great pity in this scene is that they went away. Over the deafening silence of their own guilt and shame they too might have heard God's word of grace and life that in Jesus Christ had drawn near to them.

As her accusers departed, Christ and the woman were left alone. In her guilt and shame she stood before the Word of God incarnate— the Word of God "living and active, sharper than any two-edged sword, piercing until it divides soul from spirit, joints from marrow; it is able to judge the thoughts and intentions of the heart. And before him no creature is hidden, but all are naked and laid bare to the eyes of him with whom we have to do" (HEB. 4:12-13 RSV and NRSV). And everything hung on his verdict: "Neither do I condemn you" (JOHN 8:11). Why? Surely she was guilty of adultery; the story never balks at that fact. Moreover, Jesus never assumed that she was innocent, wrongly accused, misunderstood. He told her only that she was not condemned. To her he spoke—for her he became and still is God's Word of life and love, of grace and possibility: "You are my beloved child. I have called you by name; you are mine. Because you are precious to me and I love you, do not be afraid; I am with you. See, I have graven you on the palms of my hands" (ISA. 43:1, 4a, 5a; 49:16, paraphrase).

"Jesus looked up and said to her, 'Woman, where are they? Has no one condemned you?' She said, 'No one, Lord.' And Jesus said, 'Neither do I condemn you; go, and do not sin again' " (JOHN 8:10-11 RSV). Now before we too quickly hear that as Jesus' demand upon her—the condition by which she could avoid condemnation— imagine instead that he meant it, and she heard it, not as a word of demand, but as a word of confidence and possibility. Had the woman heard it as demand she probably would have fallen back, sooner or later, into adultery. No, this was a word of Christ's faith in her, of God's belief in her. "Neither do I condemn you. You are God's own child, graven on the palms of his hands. That is the deepest truth about you; that is God's verdict upon your life. Go now, claim and live on your inheritance." And penetrating that scene is that word of grace and promise out of John's prologue: "In him was life, and . . . to all who received him, . . . he gave power to become children of God" (JOHN 1:4, 12). Where the holy God is most present, there is the greatest mercy; there is the greatest compassion; and there the beams of grace and forgiveness shoot far across the gloom of guilt. There, in him, is life.

God's final word to her life, and to your life and mine, had not to do with everlasting demands, but with everlasting promises, everlasting possibilities, and everlasting arms. "Neither do I condemn you; go, and do not sin again."

V.

God believes in us; God believes in you. And underneath that claim, to guarantee it now, is the cross of Christ marking the extent to which God will go to make good on his commitment—the breadth and length and height and depth of the love of God which surpasses knowledge. God will simply not give us up, or give up on us. With God there are no hopeless cases.

This gospel, by the way, is no denial of our freedom and responsibility in this matter of faith in God and obedience to God. We are indeed free to reject God, to ignore God, to run away from God, to despise God, to deny God's existence. We are free to go to hell if that is our decision. Even if we make our bed in hell, however, we are not free from the God who, having graven us on the palms of his hands, descends into hell in order to make good his claim upon us. In a story about Joseph Parker, minister of London's City Temple in the late nineteenth century, he once dreamed of meeting an angel, who said, "What do you think of the cross?" Parker answered, "The cross to me is marvelous and dear, because it is a sign of Christ's dying for my sin and of my cleansing from my evil." The angel replied, "That is what it is to you; but to us who have been from all eternity to all eternity, the cross is the secret of the heart of God, and it has been there all along."

A modern painting by Salvador Dali, from a drawing attributed to St. John of the Cross, shows a gap in the sky above the earth, and in the gap a cross, tilted, so that the one on the cross can look down on our world and our life. The wood of the cross is still there, as well as the nails; but the wood now is merged into infinity, and the nails have gone clear through the wood into the hands and heart and life of God. That painting is a commentary on our text, which word became flesh and dwelt among us, full of grace and truth:

I will not forget you. Behold, I have
graven you on the palms of my hands.

Notes

1. This "unauthorized sequel" to the parable of the Prodigal Son was suggested to me by my friend and teacher, Balmer H. Kelly, former professor of biblical theology at Union Theological Seminary in Virginia.

2. See Arthur John Gossip, *The Interpreter's Bible*, vol. 8, G. A. Buttrick, ed. (Nashville: Abingdon-Cokesbury Press, 1952), 593.

6
Your Light Has Come
The Man Born Blind

TWO READINGS:
Psalm 77
John 9:1-41

> Your way was through the sea,
>   your path, through the mighty waters;
>   yet your footprints were unseen.   PS. 77:19

> "As long as I am in the world, I am the light of the
> world."   JOHN 9:5

HOW DO WE discern the presence and activity of God in the events of life? Despite the glib assurances of much popular religion and the gushing testimonies that dominate television's "Christian" talk shows, so-called, this remains one of faith's most difficult questions for thoughtful men and women. To read Psalm 77 is to discover that, sadly, it has ever been so. Looking back to the Exodus—the pivotal, definitive event in Old Testament history wherein God delivered Israel from Egyptian bondage "with a mighty hand and an outstretched arm" (DEUT. 26:8)—the psalmist confesses that even there it was not easy to understand just how God was present.

> Your way was through the sea,
>   your path, through the mighty waters;
>   yet your footprints were unseen.   PS. 77:19

Surely many of us have thought the same kind of thing, some of us in events of recent days, while for others the questions reach back over bygone weeks and months and years. Not only is it difficult to understand why things happen as they do, but also sometimes we are hard put to trace in them the footprints of a loving God. "We knew you were there," the psalmist confesses to God, "but for the life of us we could not at the time see where or how."

> Your way was through the sea,
>   your path, through the mighty waters;
>   yet your footprints were unseen.

I.

People handle, or mishandle, the issue of God's presence amid the difficulties of life in various ways. Some opt for an impersonal fatalism: "Whatever will be, will be." That, however, is the ultimate denial of God's presence and purpose in human affairs. It offers no strength for our living, no help in our striving, no hope for our dying. G. K. Chesterton is reported to have said that the truth of an idea is reflected in its capacity to be used as an oath for swearing, and that the shallowness of much of life is revealed when, in a crisis, all a person can say is, "Oh, my goodness!" or "My word!" No, we need more than that—more than "goodness," more than "my word." Blessed is the man or woman who, out of great joy or need or sorrow, can pray, "Thank God!" "So help me, God!" "My God, my God, why . . . ?!"

Another response to the issue of God's presence amid the difficulties of life is a kind of heartless theism that attributes suffering to God's willful, or even punitive, intention. Something like this lay behind the disciples' question about the man's blindness in the ninth chapter of John. "Rabbi, who sinned, this man or his parents, that he was born blind?" It was a natural question for that culture where illness and physical suffering were understood as divine judgment. The disciples assumed that God had caused the affliction as just punishment for sin. All they asked was: "Whose sin was it; his parents or his own?"

But Jesus would have none of that. "Neither," he answered, thus lifting the weight of guilt from this poor family burdened enough already without having bad theology multiply their misery. There is no moral meaning to this man's blindness, Jesus said in effect. Not that his birth and blindness were outside the control and purpose of God—not at all. Consider, in fact, how his blindness might become transparent to the sustaining presence and the healing power and the redeeming grace of God. Another time, in Luke's Gospel (LUKE 13:1-5), when asked about some people who were killed when a tower fell in Siloam, a section of Jerusalem, Jesus answered, "Were they worse offenders than all the others who dwell in Jerusalem? I tell you, no!" Do not try to relate natural evil and moral meaning. Do not ask whether people killed in a flood or a blizzard are more guilty, more sinful, than others. "I tell you, no!" Ask how in this calamity the powerful grace and gracious power of God might come to light. Do not, however, correlate it to a merciless, graceless understanding of God's way with his children, so that it ceases to be a calamity—that is wrong; that is presumptuous; that is blasphemous! "Neither this man nor his parents sinned," said Jesus. "He was born blind so that God's works [God's presence and power and purpose] might be revealed in him" (JOHN 9:3).

There follows next a statement that, for John, is the interpretive key both to the healing of the blindness and, even more, to the mystery of Jesus himself. Jesus continued:

> "As long as I am in the world, I am the light of the
> world." JOHN 9:5

If the psalmist speaks of the hidden presence of God, John stands Jesus before us as the one in whom God meets and addresses us, *in person*. Indeed, as we have seen in Jesus' encounter with Nicodemus, and with the Samaritan woman, and with the woman caught in adultery, so also here the magnificent prologue to John's Gospel fairly inserts itself: "In him was life, and the life was the light of all people. The light shines in the darkness, . . ." (JOHN 1:4-5).

John is saying that in this one who declares, "I am the light of the world"—in what he says and in what he does and in who he is—the God who from the foundation of the world has pledged himself to us draws near and takes his place beside us. Paul echoes John when he says, "For it is the God who said, 'Let light shine out of darkness,' who has shone in our hearts to give the light of the knowledge of the glory of God *in the face of Jesus Christ*" (2 COR. 4:6).

So it is that when life reaches its depths, we are not thrust back on "My word!" but are upheld by *the Word* dwelling among us, full of grace and truth. We are not left to wring our hands and whimper, "Oh goodness!" but are invited to lift our hearts and sing:

> O God, our help in ages past,
>   Our hope for years to come,
> Be Thou our guard while life shall last,
>   And our eternal home!

"O God, Our Help in Ages Past"
THE PRESBYTERIAN HYMNAL, #210

II.

"As long as I am in the world, I am the light of the world." The question is, can you and I believe that? Do we? Dare we? Nothing in the story would make you think that believing could be an easy business. The blind man himself came only gradually and haltingly to understanding and confession. His healing did not suddenly make everything clear; it did not issue immediately in faith and worship. In fact, throughout the Gospels, the miracle stories are told not so much to create faith as to testify in faith, and often in retrospect, to the mysterious presence and power of God in this Jesus. The miracle stories serve not to dispel the mystery of God in Christ, but to underscore it. They remind us of the contingency of our universe, the dependence of our lives, the openness of our world and of human existence to the presence and power of God whose Word brings order out of chaos, and whose Word made flesh in Jesus Christ continues to overcome chaos with meaning and purpose, brokenness with wholeness, darkness with light, death with life.

If we find the miracle stories a problem for faith, are we so different from the characters in the stories themselves? Notice in our story, the man, now healed of his blindness, at first referred only to "the man called Jesus." Then, under pressure of the Pharisees' questioning, he was willing to go so far as to call Jesus "a prophet." He finally allowed himself the very dangerous admission that Jesus was "from God." Even at the end of the story, when he had been cast out of the synagogue, and when Jesus found him and asked: "Do you believe in the Son of Man?" the man answered, "And who is he, sir? Tell me, so that I may believe in him." In his inability to see, even now, was he so different from the psalmist? From us?

> Your way was through the sea,
>   your path, through the mighty waters;
>   yet your footprints were unseen.

Blind from birth, his eyes now opened, he still could not see, did not understand that in this "man called Jesus" God had come to him and he had been with God. John seems to be suggesting that the door of recognition (call it the door of faith, if you will) cannot be opened from our side. It can be opened only from God's side.

> He answered, "And who is he, sir? Tell me, so that
> I may believe in him." Jesus said to him, "You
> have seen him, and the one speaking with you is
> he." He said, "Lord, I believe." And he worshiped
> him.   JOHN 9:36-38

Even faith is a gift of God—one of the ways God mysteriously provides for us to keep us from falling, even when we cannot see his footprints in the mighty waters, and even though we often do not recognize him when he brings his grace and mercy to us in person.

III.

In Jesus' encounter with the man born blind, John illustrates his earlier claim that "the light shines in the darkness, and the darkness . . ." (JOHN 1:5). Now let's stop here a moment, in mid-sentence as it were. The next word is something of a puzzle in Greek. It is the Greek verb *katalambano*, meaning: to lay hold of, to grasp, to obtain, to take possession of, to overtake, to overcome, to seize, to comprehend, to understand, to perceive.

English translations have tried now one meaning, now another. The Revised Standard Version renders it: "The light shines in the darkness, and the darkness has not, or did not (NRSV), *overcome* it." J. B. Phillips' paraphrase is more poetic: "The light is still shining in the darkness, for the darkness has *never put it out.*" The Jerusalem Bible calls it: ". . . a light the darkness *could not overpower.*" In all of these is a note of victory of the light over darkness—a note of hope.

A somewhat different note is sounded in the King James Version: "And the darkness *comprehended* it not." There, in our present understanding of the word *comprehend*, the sense is more a judgment upon the world's failure to see, understand, and receive the light. The New English Bible echoes the Moffatt translation: ". . . and the darkness has never *mastered* it." *The New Testament in Braid Scots* reads delightfully: "The Licht glintit throwe the mirk! But the mirk *failed to tak haud o't.*"

With our hankering after precision and textual accuracy, we want to know which translation is closest to the truth. Is this a word of judgment or hope? The truth is, all translations are legitimate, and both meanings are accurate. Christ as the light shining in the darkness is both our judgment and our hope.

The light is still shining in the darkness, and the darkness has not comprehended or paid heed or taken hold with any understanding—that is our judgment. Like the Pharisees, we grope along in the darkness of our piety and pride, our violence and greed, our anxiety and fear, insisting self-confidently and self-righteously that we can see just fine, thank you.

However, neither has the darkness overcome the light nor taken possession of it nor extinguished it—the darkness had never put it out. God's patient and persistent grace keeps shining in our darkness—that is our eternal hope.

IV.

So where does that leave us? What can the Christian say about the presence of God amid the difficulties of life, about the light of

God's gracious presence and power shining into the darkness of our world that will not take heed and cannot extinguish it? One thing we can say has to do with our life in the world, and another has to do with the God who made that world and us, and who, in Jesus Christ, has claimed us as his own possession.

One thing we freely admit, and with which Jesus himself lived willingly and without protest, is that human existence in this world is both free and limited. We are free, but we are also finite, limited creatures, and we can be both beneficiaries and victims of this freedom and these limits. Under certain conditions accidents do happen, often with tragic and heartbreaking consequences. We hear the news reports of an airplane crash or an automobile accident; a tornado roars out of the sky, a hurricane off of the ocean; a river floods and devastates people and property over a vast area; a young woman is struck down by a freak injury that leaves her paralyzed; a virus attacks a young man's immune system and, after a long and courageous struggle, he dies; a child is born blind, as if nature, cold and impersonal, were saying, "I care nothing for your hopes and dreams, and there is no one beyond me who does." Moreover, by certain decisions taken and actions entered upon, human beings can cause pain and suffering in their own lives and in the lives of others. In these days of drug and alcohol abuse, newborn infants can show signs of a parent's addiction. Physical and emotional abuse in families shows up again and again—the sins of the fathers visited upon the children, and upon the children's children. We are punished often enough *by* our sins and the sins of others. We do not need to fall into the disciples' mistake of attributing suffering to God's punishment *for* our sins.

Christian faith, however, is able to see past the impersonal working of nature, and the willful violence of human beings, to the merciful heart of God. This is the deepest meaning of Jesus' word in John 9:5, "As long as I am in the world, I am the light of the world." In Jesus Christ, God is with us as the light even in the heart of darkness—the darkness of sin and guilt, the darkness of personal suffering, the darkness of death. In Jesus Christ, his eternal and beloved Son, God has thrust himself into the deepest darkness of the human condition. God takes our crippling guilt upon himself.

God takes the agony of our grief into his own heart. God takes our brokenness, in whatever form—our tortured and confused minds, our cancerous bodies, our fragmented relationships, our empty, broken hearts—God takes our brokenness and makes it his own even as we are his own. This means that nothing happens in this world that can ever take us out of God's presence or separate us from God's love—"neither death, nor life, . . . nor things present, nor things to come"—ever (ROM. 8:38-39). Accidents, circumstances, personal and family tragedies, as real and devastating and painful as they are, never get the last word. God has the last word, and that Word became flesh and dwelt among us in Jesus Christ—Immanuel—God with us in life and death and destiny.

To trust one's life to the God who meets us in Jesus Christ is not to believe that only good things will come our way, or that God will always order life on our terms. It is rather to know, in times of uncertainty and fear and sorrow such as many of us have known, that God is not far off, that whether in life or in death we and those whom we love are in God's omnicompetent hands, that darkness does not speak last but that God upholds us, sustains us, accompanies us through the valley of every shadow. Because in Jesus Christ God comes to us and stands with us even in the worst and most painful things, we are given faith that through the fabric of tragedy and trouble God is at work in us, for us; that our lives are in God's hands; and that even when we fall, we fall into the arms of our waiting Father. To trust one's life to this God who, in Jesus Christ, has the last word is to rest our grief in God's compassion, our hopes in God's promises, our fears in God's faithfulness, our pain in God's tender mercy, and our lives and the lives of our dear ones in God's steadfast love. God never lets us go, but holds us in everlasting arms.

V.

Your way was through the sea,
  your path, through the mighty waters;
  yet your footprints were unseen.

"As long as I am in the world, I am the light of the world."

In the life, crucifixion and resurrection of Jesus Christ, God has left visible footprints on the face of the earth. We trust that in spite of everything else those footprints belong to a God who can be worshiped and trusted, who can be questioned and argued with, but who in any case will write the final chapter to the human story, and will ever remain with, hold to, and provide for his children.

7
Facing the Last Enemy
Lazarus

TWO READINGS:
Ezekiel 37:1-14
John 11:1-44

He said to me, "Mortal, can these bones live?" I
answered, "O Lord GOD, you know." Then he said
to me, "Prophesy to these bones, and say to them:
O dry bones, hear the word of the LORD. Thus says
the Lord GOD to these bones: I will cause breath to
enter you, and you shall live. I will lay sinews on
you, and will cause flesh to come upon you, and
cover you with skin, and put breath in you, and
you shall live; and you shall know that I am the
LORD." EZEK. 37:3-6

Jesus said . . . , "I am the resurrection and the life.
Those who believe in me, even though they die,
will live." JOHN 11:25

The last enemy to be destroyed is death.
1 COR. 15:26

OUR ENCOUNTERS along the way of the cross next bring us to
the strange and moving story of the raising of Lazarus. In considering
Jesus' encounters—with the tempter in the wilderness, with Nicodemus by night, with the woman of Samaria and the woman caught
in adultery, with the man born blind—we have seen what happens

to the power of evil, to the despair and loneliness and tragedy that blight human existence when the Word becomes flesh and dwells among us full of grace and truth, full of light and life. These encounters tell of God's entering into the heart of life—into the depths of the human condition—and thus they prepare us for the passion and resurrection wherein we discover the breadth and length and height and depth of the love of God in Christ Jesus our Lord.

Here in the story of Lazarus, Jesus faced the ultimate challenge—what Paul calls "the last enemy." Tortured Nicodemus could always press his quest for assurance of divine favor through one more night. The Samaritan woman at the well could always wait one tomorrow more for love to find her. The woman taken in adultery could carry her load of guilt a few steps farther along. What was one more day to a man blind from his birth? They all had a future toward which to live and hope. But what is to hope for at the sealed door of a fresh tomb? The Lazarus story is about death, about fear, about anguish and tears, about pain and grief so intense that nothing could make it go away.

I.

As the scene unfolds, John skillfully captures our discomfort, our revulsion, our fear in face of death. For example, there is Jesus' initial hesitation: "After having heard that Lazarus was ill, he stayed two days longer in the place where he was" (JOHN 11:6). In the other encounters, there had been no holding back, no reluctance to become involved with Nicodemus, the two women, with the blind man. Here, however, when Mary and Martha send for him to come to Bethany to the sickbed—the deathbed—of his friend Lazarus, there is on the part of Jesus this studied procrastination, if not out-and-out reluctance, about going to him. Can we not detect a note of embarrassed confusion running through John's account? It sounds as if John is at great pains to explain away this delay.

Why the hesitation? Could it be that we are given here a glimpse of Jesus' true humanity? Could it be that this one who, as the early theologians would express it, was "in his humanity of the same reality as are we" (definition of Chalcedon, 451 A.D.) reacts to death as we do, with revulsion? For Jesus, death was an enemy—the last enemy. The grief, the fear, the emptiness we experience when death invades our lives and claims a loved one were as real and painful for Jesus as they are for us. For Jesus, as well as for Mary and Martha and the other mourners, it was at the point and in the hour of death that faith in God was taken to the final extremity. Perhaps Jesus reacted as he did, not from a lack of compassion, but from a genuine anguish of soul—a mixture of anger and fear, aversion and disgust, grief and resentment.[1]

By the time Jesus arrived in Bethany, Lazarus' body had already been in the tomb four days. Lazarus had been Jesus' friend—his beloved friend[2]—and when, with Mary and Martha, Jesus came to his grave we are told that he wept, that he was deeply moved, that he was troubled. No doubt he was troubled by the mixture of love and resentment in the sisters' words: "Lord, if you had been here, my brother would not have died!" They both said it, and just that way. Surely he was troubled by the comments of the bystanders, which probably reminded him of what he had already said to himself: "Could not he who opened the eyes of the blind man have kept this man from dying?" Possibly he was troubled, and even a little angry, about God, the Author and Preserver of life, who could not, or would not, or did not preserve Lazarus' life, and whose sovereignty was, and is, called into question by death as by nothing else.

Lazarus died, and being deeply moved in spirit and troubled, Jesus wept. Sir Walter Scott described the aching emptiness when his wife died: "A kind of cloud of stupidity hangs about me, as if all were unreal that men seem to be doing and talking."[3] John presents a picture taken straight from life: the initial hesitation, the grief, the tears, the resentment, the revulsion in face of death, the sense in the pit of your stomach and the depth of your soul that everything has come undone—the experience of the absence of God. All this makes up the deafening silence that surrounds us and the overwhelming emptiness that grips us when faith faces the final enemy.[4]

II.

As a sloping beach sometimes plunges quickly into vast deeps, so in this story we suddenly find ourselves among unfathomable things. This one who wept at the grave of his friend, John keeps telling us in story after story, was God in person—the Word made flesh. In Christ, almighty God had thrust himself into human existence, had taken upon himself the totality of our condition—not just our dignity and goodness, our health and strength, but our fear and confusion, our shame and guilt, our brokenness and our dying. God who became vulnerable and weak—an infant crying in a manger bed—now, heartbroken and weeping, took his place with a grief-stricken family at the time of death.

This is no Greek hero god come down from some Olympus, well out of the storms that beat against us, easily and cheerfully playing out a charade of human life, but never really being touched by its pain and heartache. No! "The Word became flesh and lived among us," says John. Henceforth we know God as a God who, deeply moved, will be present at our funerals to weep with and to comfort those who mourn, and to bear our griefs and carry our sorrows. The Bible does not back away from the reality and fear and pain of death. The Bible does not back away from the agonizing experience of the absence of God. Without apology John shows Jesus weeping, deeply moved in spirit and troubled, as if to say: "Look, the tears that fall on the ground at Lazarus' tomb well up from the broken heart of God! See the wonder of God's compassion! See the lengths to which God has gone and continues to go in order to stand with us at the point of our deepest need—even as faith faces the last enemy."

The same love with which God numbers the hairs on our head and will not allow even a sparrow to fall to the ground and be lost also moves God to tears over the death of even one beloved child. This is God with us in death, in the death of those we love, going down with us into the darkness of God-forsakenness, descending into hell with us, and so showing us what it means that we are children of God. This is the astounding claim of the gospel: that in Christ God knows what it means to look death in the eye, knows what it means both to die and to suffer the death of one beloved above all others. (And those of us who have loved and do love, however imperfectly, know that would be worse than our own dying.)

Like the sisters and friends of Lazarus, therefore, we listen to the gospel for some word of God's presence. We listen, perhaps not as well as we should, to the Word read and proclaimed, never as well as it should be. Often we listen in spite of ourselves, but we listen because we begin to understand that when faith faces the last enemy, then "God" is not an answer we can conveniently produce to fill that void. In fact, there is no answer as such that we can come up with, no matter what popular religion and popular psychology and the cults of self-help claim. When faith faces the last enemy— when to us God, for all the world, is absent, there is one possible solution: God must break through to us in person; God must turn absence into presence, darkness into light, silence into speech, and death into life. Apart from God's coming to us, we are alone, and undone.

III.

We have acknowledged the deafening silence and the terrible emptiness and the dull pain that confront us, and the inadequacy of our easy answers when faith faces the last enemy. It is time now to break that silence—time for a word, the Word. Everything that makes up the silence and pain has been faced: the hesitation, the grief, the tears, the resentment, the shakenness in the depth of the soul, the sense of the absence of God. Now it is time to break the silence. Now it is time for a word, for the Word who was with God in the beginning, and who was God, and who is God.

The story continues:

> Then Jesus, deeply moved again, came to the
> tomb; it was a cave, and a stone lay upon it.
> JOHN 11:38 RSV

Just as David had faced Goliath, an enemy he and everyone else evidently recognized to be superior, but whom he was resolutely determined to destroy, so Jesus confronted the closed grave, the corruption which had already set in, the sealed finality of death. What did he mean by his promise: "Your brother will rise again"

(JOHN 11:23)? Did he mean only the vague, popular doctrine of a general resurrection of which the Pharisees were the leading proponents? That was Martha's assumption when she said, "I know that he will rise again in the resurrection on the last day" (JOHN 11:24).

No! "I am . . . ," Jesus said. There is that "I am" again which dominates the Fourth Gospel, just as the strange name of God, "I am who I am," dominates the Old Testament. "I am," Jesus said, not merely life, but because I am the presence and power of life in a world given up to death, "I am the resurrection and the life . . . !" This is the word Jesus flings even into the face of death. Its tense is both present and future; and the mood of the scene itself both indicative, pointing to an accomplished fact, and imperative, calling us to trust.

Here John confronts us with the dramatic unity of the Word and act of God. Jesus spoke right into the freshly sealed grave of Lazarus, crying with a loud voice. "Lazarus, come out!" This is the battle of God for the cause of humanity—for Lazarus, for you, for me, for our dearest loved ones, all of us God's children ordained by our Father/Creator for eternal life and not for eternal death. Furthermore, when in the grip of death Lazarus heard the word and did as he was commanded, Jesus said, in both symbol and fact of God's victory in this battle: "Unbind him, and let him go"!

The mystery of who Jesus was begins to unfold in this dramatic and almost breathtaking story: the Word of God, God's coming to us and being for us in person, even when faith faces the last enemy.

If we ask why John includes such macabre details as a grieving family, a sealed tomb, and the resuscitation of an already decomposing and redolent corpse, the answer must be that those are the trappings of death which are to us most dreadfully real and stark. That is where the battle is joined then, and where the meaning of Christ for us is dramatically underscored.

> "I am the resurrection and the life. Those who
> believe in me, even though they die, will live."
>
> JOHN 11:25

IV.

Perhaps it is futile, even stupid, to attempt to comment on a passage so majestic and unfathomable. It has the quality more of music than of words. It sets before our minds truth too deep, too profound to be expressed in stammering human speech. However, even as we fumble around the outer edge of this strange text and story we begin to see just Who stands with us and fights for us and holds on to us when we face the last enemy.

Woven into the entire drama are the mysterious presence and power of God at a time when God seemed most to be absent. That is the overarching theme and the rock-bottom meaning of the story. The raising of Lazarus is not an Easter story. Resurrection is not primarily about miracles like the temporary revival of Lazarus. If it were, we would spend our whole life in a frenzy, asking God to postpone just one more time the griefs and losses that belong to us as human beings. No, it is clear that Lazarus will die again at some later time, and will be mourned.

The raising of Lazarus, as John records it here, takes place as a sign! It is a dramatic sign that this one who says "I am the resurrection and the life" both tells the truth, and is the Truth. In that Truth we live; and in that Life, death itself, including our own death and the death of those we love, is overcome. Death is not avoided; death is overcome.

Over against the stark reality of death, says this strange story, God faithfully utters the word of life. Who else could utter it? That word which called Lazarus forth from the tomb is, Genesis tells us, the same word that called the world and life into being, and which Ezekiel reminds us can make even dry bones live! So it is that later on another writer named John, in this same New Testament tradition, provides a concluding word to the New Testament:

> And I heard a great voice from the throne saying,
> "Behold, the dwelling of God is with human
> beings. He will dwell with them as their God; they
> shall be his people, and God himself will be with
> them; he will wipe away every tear from their
> eyes, and death shall be no more, neither shall

> there be mourning nor crying nor pain any more,
> for . . . I am the Alpha and the Omega, the
> beginning and the end.   REV. 21:3-4, 6, paraphrase

The victory does not come easy though, nor is the gift of life cheap. John tells us that it was precisely this giving back to Lazarus his life that set in motion the events that cost Jesus his own life.

> Many of the Jews therefore, who had come with
> Mary and had seen what Jesus did, believed in
> him. But some of them went to the Pharisees and
> told them what he had done. So the chief priests
> and the Pharisees called a meeting of the council,
> and said, "What are we to do? This man is
> performing many signs. If we let him go on like
> this, everyone will believe in him, and the Romans
> will come and destroy both our holy place and our
> nation." . . . So from that day on they planned to
> put him to death.   JOHN 11:45-53

On our journey along the way of the cross that eventually leads to Easter, we trace a line from the tomb of Lazarus through the Garden of Gethsemane to the Place of the Skull, and from there to the empty tomb. We trace a line from the tomb of Lazarus to Gethsemane where, in the voice of one struggling in the night with his doubts and fears, we are given assurance that in our own doubts and fears and dark nights of the soul, we are not alone. We trace a line from the tomb of Lazarus to the Place of the Skull where, in one dying on a cross, we see God with us in our pilgrimage through the valley of the shadow of death. We trace a line from the sealed tomb of Lazarus to the empty tomb of Jesus, carried along by those words which only God himself could speak:

> "I am the resurrection and the life."

Until once again, in the wonder of his passion and in the mystery of his resurrection we know, even when we face the last enemy, that our lives and the lives of those we love are "hid with Christ in God" (COL. 3:3 RSV), safe in God's keeping for time and for eternity.

Notes

1. Compare Jesus' sense of revulsion here to the account in Mark 1:40-45 of the healing of the leper, where the Greek text in verses 41 and 43 suggests that Jesus reacts to the leper more in indignation than in compassion. Aversion would be a very natural and very human response to a leper who did not keep his distance, but who violated a strict taboo by rushing into the presence of another. This interpretation of the passage would be in keeping with other instances (e.g., Mark 1:21-28; 2:1-12; 4:35-41) in which Mark underscores the humanity of Jesus who nevertheless is the one in whom the presence and power of God are present and at work.

2. There is a theory that Lazarus was the "beloved disciple." (See John 11:3, 5, 36; 12:2; 13:23.) This would add poignancy to Peter's question in John 21:20-23. See F. V. Filson, "Who Was the Beloved Disciple?" *Journal of Biblical Literature* 68 (March 1949): 83–88.

3. See Gossip, *Interpreter's Bible*, 643.

4. It may well be that John does not report Jesus' agony in Gethsemane, as do the other evangelists, because for John this confrontation with death at Lazarus' tomb *is* "Gethsemane." But see also John 12:27-36, another Gethsemane-type reference in the Fourth Gospel.

8
When God Steps In
Thomas

TWO READINGS:
Ecclesiastes 1:12—2:11
John 20:1-31

> I saw all the deeds that are done under the sun;
> and see, all is vanity and a chasing after wind.
> What is crooked cannot be made straight,
> and what is lacking cannot be counted.
>
> ECCLES. 1:14-15

> Jesus came and stood among them.   JOHN 20:19

EASTER IS NOT something that happened once. It keeps on happening. That morning in the garden, Mary Magdalene had found the tomb empty: "They have taken away my Lord, and I do not know where they have laid him" (JOHN 20:13). When she turned around, Jesus was standing there, unrecognized until he called her name, "Mary!" John's earlier image of Christ as the Good Shepherd comes remarkably to light: "The sheep hear his voice as he calls by name those that belong to him" (see JOHN 10:3).

That evening, fearing for their own safety, the disciples huddled together behind locked doors. We can imagine that they had posted a lookout to watch for a shadow or listen for a footfall on the stairway.

Suddenly, without warning, undeterred by their precautions, as John tells it, "Jesus came and stood among them." "Peace be with you," he said. It was the gift he had promised them that last time they had been together, when everything seemed to be coming apart at the seams and they had been so anxious and afraid: "Peace I leave with you; my peace I give to you; not as the world gives do I give to you. Let not your hearts be troubled, neither let them be afraid" (JOHN 14:27 RSV).

There had been other appearances. Two disciples were walking on the road to Emmaus when a stranger fell into step and into conversation with them, and even joined them for supper. "When he was at the table with them," as Luke recounts it, "he took bread, blessed and broke it, and gave it to them. Then their eyes were opened, and they recognized him. . . . Then they told what had happened on the road, and how he had been made known to them in the breaking of the bread" (LUKE 24:30-31,35). Surely Christians cherished the stories across the years, these little communities of faith scattered about in a hostile world; because the theme that sounds again and again in the Easter proclamation reverberated in their own worship and in the experiences of their life together.

> Then Jesus came and stood among them and said,
> "Peace be with you."

Of course, believing in the resurrection was not exactly easy. Matthew tells us that even after that first Easter when, at Jesus' direction, the disciples had gathered on a mountain in Galilee, "When they saw him they worshiped him; but some doubted" (MATT. 28:17). It is significant that both worshipers and doubters were in that group to whom Jesus came and said "All authority in heaven and on earth has been given to me. Go therefore and make disciples of all nations, baptizing them in the name of the Father and of the Son and of the Holy Spirit, and teaching them to obey everything that I have commanded you. And remember, I am with you always, to the end of the age" (MATT. 28:18-20). Perhaps that is why the story of Thomas came to have a special place in the memory of the early

church. Their doubts did not exclude them from the call, the com-
mission, the promise of the risen Christ. There was room in the
church for Thomas and his tribe, the skeptical and doubting ones.

> So the other disciples told [Thomas], "We have
> seen the Lord." But he said to them, "Unless I see
> the mark of the nails in his hands, and put my
> finger in the mark of the nails and my hand in his
> side, I will not believe." JOHN 20:25

A week later, "Jesus came and stood among them and said, "Peace
to you . . . Thomas . . . put out your hand. . . ." Can you hear the
reassuring echo? Do not fear, for I have redeemed you; I have called
you by name, you are mine" (ISA. 43:1). You, Israel; you, Andrew,
Peter, James, John; you, Nicodemus; you, Samaritan woman there
at the well; you, woman caught in adultery; you, man born blind;
you, Lazarus; you, Mary; you, Thomas—you are mine! Resurrection
is not just for those for whom faith is easy. Easter makes room for
Thomas too.

I.

Recalling the sermons he had listened to, a Columbia University
student said that most of them left him thinking, "That isn't true;
but I wish it were."[1] That is Thomas for you, and there is no telling
how many Thomases there have been in every generation, and how
many there are among us today—I have been there myself, more
than once. When Easter happens, however, and keeps on happening—when God steps in, when Jesus stands among us—all of
us Thomases finally have to consider that what sounds and seems
"too good to be true" just might be too good *not* to be true.

For one thing, Easter is God's way of saying something that
desperately needs to be said about the kind of world we live in, and
about the life we are involved with. Because God created this world,
because God rules this world with truth and grace, because God is
at work in this world to accomplish his sovereign purpose, it is
therefore a world in which sin, evil, and death, as real as they are,
do not have the final power or the last word. God's world is a world

over which an empty cross has been raised as a sign that nobody can be done to death by either violence or vengeance, disease or disaster, accident or design without there arising from deep within the universe—from within the very heart of God—a great protest and an unremitting resolve to put things right. This world, including your life and the lives of those you love, belongs to the God who numbers the very hairs of your head, who does not allow even a sparrow to fall to the ground and be lost, and who meets oppression with exodus, Good Friday's cross with Easter's empty tomb, and death's dark shadow of despair with the hope and comfort of resurrection.

Resurrection means that something or Someone else is at work in this world other than our science and technology, our commerce and politics, our intrigues and ideologies, our striving and attainment—all of those things that leave the writer of Ecclesiastes so disillusioned. Resurrection means that over against the verdict "all is vanity and a striving after wind," which Ecclesiastes pronounces on human existence; over against Gethsemane's agony and Judas' betrayal and Peter's denial; over against Caiaphas' accusations and Pilate's sentence and the shouts of "Crucify!"; over against Calvary's cross and the God-forsakenness on that gallows and that grave in Joseph's garden stand God's resourcefulness, God's power, God's sovereign and invincible purpose that can bring Christmas out of a cowshed, and twenty centuries of Christian faith out of a tomb.[2] God's Easter response to Good Friday underscores something that desperately needed to be said about this world in which we live.

II.

Easter is also God's way of saying something that needs to be said about human beings—about Mary and the disciples and Thomas, about you and about me—about our own death and our own life. Resurrection makes possible a certain courage in facing our own death and the death of those we love. At its deepest level, the resurrection of Jesus Christ means that God is faithful and that as God's children, we can trust God to preserve us and to do with our life and with the lives of our loved ones what a loving, just, and gracious God will do. Resurrection does not save us from dying; it does, however, save us from the dominion of death. Resurrection does not keep us from "having to die"; it does mean that God keeps his own in life and in death—that in and through and beyond our dying we are held fast in the heart and hand of God. We are given no details of the life everlasting, nor should we pretend that our faith and knowledge are sufficient to cover all our anxiety. At the same time, resurrection is God's promise to complete what we cannot complete for ourselves, and to keep us and sustain us in life and death and destiny.

Resurrection, however, is not simply a word for the future, relevant only to our dying. Resurrection is God's sign and seal upon our living. Resurrection has to do not only with God's promise to preserve our lives; resurrection has to do with God's power to *direct* our lives. Resurrection is not merely God's correcting and making up for what has gone wrong; resurrection is God's confidence in those whom he has created, claimed, and called to be about his business.

The disciples cowered in that room as night fell on that first Easter day. We can imagine that besides being afraid and despondent, they were perhaps ashamed of having denied and forsaken Jesus, and possibly a little resentful of his having failed them. Then

> Jesus came and stood among them and said, . . .
> "Peace be with you. As the Father has sent me, so
> I send you."   JOHN 20:19,21

"God has failed neither of us," Jesus said in effect, "nor are you going to fail me. Whatever you have done and whatever you have been, I still trust you and believe in you." Christ startled the disciples out of their disillusionment and belittling of themselves as proven failures by holding to his choice of them and committing his cause to them. "As the Father has sent me, even so I send you." These words reminded them of something he had said to them earlier: "You did not choose me but I chose you. And I appointed you to go and bear fruit, fruit that will last" (JOHN 15:16). They heard him saying to them, "Look, my choice of you was no accident; I knew what I was doing. Yes, and I have seen you at your worst: trying to make me conform to your expectations, arguing over who was

the greatest, lobbying for choice seats in the kingdom, going to
sleep in my hour of agony, betraying me, denying me, forsaking me.
And knowing all that, I reaffirm my choice of you and my confidence
in you."

You can imagine what that did for them. Suddenly, their fear
did not matter any more, or their having denied him and having
run away, or any of their flaws of faith and character; none of this
separated them from him. The only thing that mattered was that
"Jesus came and stood among them and said, 'Peace be with you.
As the Father has sent me, so I send you.'" Sounding through this
resurrection scene is the theme John introduced at the beginning of
his Gospel and reiterated time and again in scene after scene, encounter after encounter: "In him was life!" Nicodemus had heard
it, and the Samaritan woman and the woman caught in adultery
and the blind man and Mary and Martha and Lazarus and Mary
Magdalene and Thomas. At one point John captured the theme in
a sentence that is the best known in any Gospel:

> For God so loved the world that he gave his only
> Son, that whoever believes . . . [might] . . . have
> . . . life.   JOHN 3:16 RSV

At the conclusion of his Gospel, John says that he has written "that
you may believe that Jesus is the Christ, the Son of God, and that
believing you may have life in his name" (JOHN 20:31 RSV). Finally,
there is an echo in a letter that bears John's name: "See what love
the Father has given us, that we should be called children of God;
and so we are" (1 JOHN 3:1 RSV).

III.

That same Columbia University student also said he had heard
a few sermons that left him whispering to himself, "That's true; but
I wish it were not."[3] There is something unsettling about the resurrection. Resurrection means that God has taken an action after
which nothing can ever again be the same. The deepest truth of
Easter is infinitely, categorically, qualitatively different from any routine or natural event like the coming of spring. We cannot downplay

resurrection to a vague doctrine of natural immortality that we celebrate once a year when the flowers come out again and the butterflies emerge. Resurrection means that God is on the loose in our world, and that no matter what, God is going to find us and claim us as his own possession. Thomas may have understood that in a way the others did not.

The resurrection of Jesus takes us beyond the limit of human possibility. Whether it is the women standing before an empty tomb (MARK 16), or Mary Magdalene or Thomas facing the risen Christ, at that point all that constitutes the human capacity for shaping, managing, or controlling life is at an end. Human strength; human comprehension; human understanding; human imagination, intuition, feeling, expression all are powerless and can only give way before this phenomenon of which God alone can be and is the source and subject. Resurrection—God's breaking of the power of evil, sin, and death—means the end of human possibility.

For a person like Thomas, who insisted on being the final judge of what could be and what was true, the resurrection was at least as threatening as it was thrilling. He knew the discomfort, the uneasiness of being at the limit of human possibility. This is why it is especially appropriate that John makes Thomas the final witness for the disciples—for the faith of the Christian community—in his ultimate confession: "My Lord and my God!" (JOHN 20:28).

Some among us find faith as easy and natural as breathing in and breathing out. We think of the beloved disciple who believed after having seen only the empty tomb and the folded graveclothes. There is Mary Magdalene who, in her eagerness to believe, responded quickly to Christ's call. There are the disciples who were brought from deep, dark despair to new life and faith and hope when "Jesus came and stood among them." Faith for such as those comes as easily and as naturally as breathing.

There are others however who, like a person with asthma, have to fight for every breath of faith. They are the spiritual descendants of Thomas, they of the restless heart, the fretful spirit, the doubting mind. One of their number, Søren Kierkegaard, the "melancholy Dane," is reported to have prayed, "Teach me, O God, not to torture myself, not to make a martyr out of myself through stifling reflection, but rather teach me to breathe deeply in faith." It is not that people choose to be thus; indeed, even in their perplexity, they are members of the household of faith. In the person of Thomas, they take their rightful place among the disciples in that upper room to whom Christ came and spoke the word of life that is meant for even the most restless heart, even the most troubled spirit and the most skeptical mind, even the most critical intellect, even the most rebellious will.

That is why I am glad that John allows Thomas to confess the faith for us all: "My Lord and my God!" This confirms that for everyone—for all of us and for each of us—Easter is about God-in-Christ bringing us his life and his love one more time: one more time than we can doubt it, one more time than we can deny it, one more time than we can reject it.

Notes

1. Paul Scherer, *The Word God Sent* (New York: Harper and Row, 1965), 188.
2. Ibid., 190.
3. Ibid., 192.

For Further Reading

Achtemeier, Paul J. and Elizabeth. *To Save All People*. Boston: United Church Press, 1967.

Augustine of Hippo. *The City of God*. Translated by Marcus Dods. New York: Modern Library, 1950.

———. *Confessions. In the Nicene and Post-Nicene Fathers*. Vol. 1. Edited by Philip Schaff. Grand Rapids: Eerdmans, 1979.

Barrett, C. K. *The Gospel According to St. John*. 2d ed. Philadelphia: Westminster Press, 1978.

Barth, Karl. *Church Dogmatics*, Vols. 1–4. Edinburgh: T & T Clark, 1936–69.

———. *Credo*. New York: Charles Scribner's Sons, 1962.

———. *The Göttingen Dogmatics*. Vol. 1. Grand Rapids: Eerdmans, 1991.

———. *The Resurrection of the Dead*. London: Hodder & Stoughton, 1933.

———. *Witness to the Word*. Grand Rapids: Eerdmans, 1986.

———. *The Word of God and the Word of Man*. New York: Harper & Row, 1957.

Blenkinsopp, Joseph. *Ezekiel: A Commentary for Teaching and Preaching*. Louisville: John Knox Press, 1990.

Brown, Peter. *Augustine of Hippo*. Berkeley: University of California Press, 1967.

Brown, Raymond, E., S.S. *The Gospel According to John, I–XII*. Garden City: Doubleday & Company, 1966.

———. *The Gospel According to John, XIII–XXI*. Garden City: Doubleday & Company, 1970.

Brueggemann, Walter, *Genesis: A Bible Commentary for Teaching and Preaching*. Atlanta: John Knox Press, 1982.

Buechner, Frederick. *Telling the Truth: The Gospel as Tragedy, Comedy, and Fairy Tale*. New York: Harper & Row, 1977.

Crenshaw, James L. *Ecclesiastes: A Commentary*. Philadelphia: Westminster Press, 1987.

Currie, Thomas W., III. *Ambushed by Grace*. Allison Park, Pa.: Pickwick Publishers, 1993.

Dodd, C. H. *The Interpretation of the Fourth Gospel*. Cambridge: University Press, 1963.

Eichrodt, Walther. *Ezekiel: A Commentary*. London: SCM Press, 1970.

Forsyth, Peter T. *Positive Preaching and the Modern Mind*. New York: Baker Books, 1980.

Fuller, Reginald H. *The Formation of the Resurrection Narrative*. New York: Macmillan, 1971.

Gordis, Robert. *Koheleth, The Man and His World: A Study of Ecclesiastes*. 3d ed. New York: Shocken Books, 1968.

Kimel, Alvin F., Jr., ed. *Speaking the Christian God*. Grand Rapids: William B. Eerdmans, 1992.

Leith, John H. *Basic Christian Doctrine*. Louisville: Westminster/John Knox Press, 1993.

Marxsen, Willi. *The Resurrection of Jesus of Nazareth.* Philadelphia: Fortress Press, 1970.

Meilaender, Gilbert C. *Faith and Faithfulness.* Notre Dame: University of Notre Dame Press, 1991.

Miller, Patrick D. *Deuteronomy—A Commentary for Teaching and Preaching.* Louisville: John Knox Press, 1990.

Moule, C. F. D., ed. *The Significance of the Message of the Resurrection for Faith in Jesus Christ.* Naperville, Ill.: Alec R. Alleson, 1968.

Niebuhr, H. Richard. *Faith on Earth.* New Haven: Yale University Press, 1989.

————. *The Meaning of Revelation.* New York: Macmillan, 1960.

Niebuhr, Reinhold. *The Nature and Destiny of Man.* 2 vols. New York: Charles Scribner's Sons, 1964.

Outler, Albert C. *Who Trusts in God.* New York: Oxford University Press, 1968.

Rogers, John B., Jr. *The Birth of God.* Nashville: Abingdon, 1987.

Scherer, Paul. *Event in Eternity.* New York: Harper & Brothers, 1945.

————. *The Word God Sent.* New York: Harper & Row, 1965.

Schnackenburg, Rudolf. *The Gospel According to St. John.* Vols. 1–3. New York: Crossroad, 1990.

Sloyan, Gerard. *John—A Bible Commentary for Teaching and Preaching.* Atlanta: John Knox Press, 1988.

Smith, George Adam. *The Book of Isaiah, XL–LXVI.* London: Hodder & Stoughton, 1890.

Taylor, Charles. *Sources of the Self.* Cambridge: Harvard University Press, 1989.

von Rad, Gerhard. *Deuteronomy, A Commentary.* Philadelphia: Westminster Press, 1966.

————. *Genesis, A Commentary.* Philadelphia: Westminster Press, 1961.

Westermann, Claus. *Genesis 1–11.* Minneapolis: Augsburg, 1984.

————. *Genesis 12–36.* Minneapolis: Augsburg, 1985.

————. *Isaiah 40–66: A Commentary.* Philadelphia: Westminster Press, 1969.